Teaching
Basic
Skills

This b   et

Teaching Basic Skills

The Principles of Instruction

Jason M. White
UNIVERSITY OF ADELAIDE

AND

Neil Brewer
FLINDERS UNIVERSITY
OF SOUTH AUSTRALIA

Copyright © Jason M. White and Neil Brewer 1992

First published 1992 by
MACMILLAN EDUCATION AUSTRALIA PTY LTD
107 Moray Street, South Melbourne 3205
6 Clarke Street, Crows Nest 2065

Associated companies and representatives
throughout the world

National Library of Australia
cataloguing in publication data:

White, Jason M., 1954–
    Teaching basic skills: the principles of instruction.

    ISBN 0 7329 1858 8.
    ISBN 0 7329 1857 X (pbk.).

    1. Basic education. I. Brewer, Neil. II. Title.

372.011

Set in Century Old Style, Garamond and Optima
by Typeset Gallery Sdn. Bhd., Malaysia
Printed in Hong Kong

Contents

Introduction   vi
Acknowledgements   xi

Chapter 1   **Types of learning   1**
Discriminations   1
  Attention   2
Relations   5
Rules   7
Production skills   9
Conceptual understanding   10
Exercises   11

Chapter 2   **General instructional principles:**
      part 1   13
Feedback   14
  Role of feedback   14
  Using feedback   19
Mastery   23
  Pacing   27
Exercises   29

Chapter 3   **General instructional principles:**
      part 2   31
Prompting and fading   32
  Prompts   32
  Fading   41
Exercises   47

Chapter 4   **General instructional principles:**
          part 3   49
          Errorless discrimination learning   49
            Techniques   50
          Chaining   55
            Techniques   58
            More complex rules   61
          Shaping   66
          Choosing between procedures   69
          Exercises   69

Chapter 5   **A sample instructional program   71**
          Mastery aim   71
          Assumed prerequisites   71
          Types of learning   72
          Instructional methods   72
            Rules: counting rule for addition   75
            Problems of implementation   77

Chapter 6   **Adaptations for students with learning**
          problems   78
          Feedback   79
          Mastery   81
            Prompting and fading   82
            Errorless discrimination learning   83
            Chaining   84
          Conclusion   86

          Answers   87
            Chapter 1   87
            Chapter 2   89
            Chapter 3   91
            Chapter 4   94
          Glossary   102
          References   106

          Index   112

Introduction

The term basic skills encompasses skills as diverse as recognizing and naming shapes, letters and numerals, solving problems involving concepts such as more than, less than, bigger and smaller, counting and performing a variety of arithmetic operations, implementing rules of grammar in oral and written language, drawing shapes and writing letters with precision. These and many others are typically the province of the earlier years of education. Why are they important? One major reason is that mastery of these more basic skills is crucial for the learning of more advanced academic skills. Another is that efficient learning at this basic level can ensure that students experience the success that is necessary to sustain motivation for further learning.

In this book, a set of principles which underlie effective instruction of basic academic skills is described. These principles should be implemented systematically, if learning is to occur efficiently. How these principles are incorporated into actual learning activities by teachers or instructors is not the focus of the book. The specific ways in which these principles are put into practice will obviously vary from instructor to instructor, and will depend upon factors such as the nature of the teaching activities they typically use, the teaching environment, the type and number of students, etc. The important thing, however, is that the principles outlined in the ensuing chapters can be accommodated within a wide variety of teaching practices.

The book is organized into four main chapters, and two which expand on these. Chapter 1 identifies the four categories of learning involved in the acquisition of basic academic skills. These four categories are referred to as discriminations, relations, rules or procedures, and production skills. Chapters 2, 3 and 4 focus on methods by which these different categories of learning can be achieved.

In Chapter 2, the way to provide student feedback (both instructional and motivational) is discussed, and how reliance on that feedback can be reduced as student learning advances. Also in this chapter is described what is involved in mastery learning, that is, where student progression is contingent on the mastery of more basic levels. Here two major issues are covered: one is concerned with achieving the precise specification of what the student must learn, the other major issue is concerned with how the rate of student progression is determined by instructors.

In the next two chapters (Chapters 3 and 4) are stated the methods by which structured progression can be achieved. In essence, this means that students progress through gradually more difficult stages of learning in a manner designed to ensure throughout that they experience success and receive positive feedback. In Chapter 3 the principles of prompting and fading are outlined. These terms encompass a set of techniques that can be used across the four main categories of learning (i.e., discriminations, relations, rules and production skills) in order to ensure that the student succeeds from the outset. Reviewed are the basic principles associated with using various prompting techniques such as instructions, models, matching-to-sample, physical guidance, pointers, highlighting and known equivalents. This is followed by a discussion of fading procedures. These procedures should be used to reduce the intensity of prompts in order to ensure that students continue to experience success when performing independently.

Chapter 4 deals with those methods of achieving structured progression which are specific to several particular categories of learning. First, the application of what are known as errorless discrimination learning procedures to the teaching of discriminations and relations is discussed, with three major techniques being illustrated. Then the application of chaining techniques which can be used to teach rules or procedures is considered. Finally, Chapter 4 describes how a procedure called shaping can be used to teach production skills.

Chapter 5 illustrates how the various principles may be integrated when designing an instructional program. For one particular academic skill is provided a detailed worked example which incorporates mastery aims, feedback provision and withdrawal, prompting and fading, and procedures for achieving structured progression which are appropriate for the particular categories of learning involved.

The approach taken in Chapters 1–4 is that the systematic application of the principles outlined in those chapters will enable all students to learn. But, for some individuals, the methods outlined will require minor but important adaptations or refinements if they are to be maximally effective. These adaptations are dealt with in Chapter 6, where particular attention is given to the instruction of individuals who have general or specific learning problems — that is, those individuals with varying degrees of intellectual disability, or those who experience difficulties with particular areas of learning.

At the end of Chapter 6 a glossary of technical terms is provided. Those terms that are included in the Glossary are made **bold** where they first appear in the text.

While it may be argued that the principles described in this book are crucial for the learning of more basic skills, it is not suggested that other principles are unimportant. Instead, as students progress to more advanced learning, there is no doubt that other principles assume increasing significance. For example, while in these chapters procedures are advocated which ensure that students experience success throughout, working out solutions to problems through the analysis of incorrect solutions is often a key part of more advanced learning. Likewise, instruction of more advanced academic skills often involves encouraging students to develop more general learning strategies that will provide them with greater flexibility and independence when they are placed in new learning situations.

Finally, here are a few suggestions about how this text might be used. It is suitable both for students training to teach in regular education settings and for those training in special education. Student exercises (accompanied by appropriate answers) are provided with Chapters 1 to 4, and these should allow instructors to assess directly whether or not students can implement the principles set out in these chapters. For example, these exercises could be used as a starting point for tutorial discussion, and as a basis for the development of further exercises of the same type. The actual examples given are perhaps more typical of learning situations encountered by younger children. Nevertheless, the content of the questions can readily be adapted by the imaginative instructor to provide exercises for students training to work with different populations (e.g., developmentally disabled adults).

Acknowledgements

Several undergraduate classes used initial drafts of this book as a course text. The input of these students was invaluable in shaping the final product. Our thanks to Debbie Harvey for meticulous typing of the initial draft, and to Carol McNally and Marie Baker for their careful work on the later versions. Finally, we dedicate this book to Mary White and Kathryn Brewer for their support and forbearance.

Jason M. White
Neil Brewer

Chapter 1
Types of learning

This chapter outlines the different types of learning which are involved in the acquisition of basic academic skills. A number of different categories are identified and discussed. These categories are **discriminations**, **relations**, **rules** and **production skills**. While each category appears to be relatively simple, hopefully this book will make it apparent that very sophisticated material can be learned through the combination of such processes. Finally, in this chapter is demonstrated the relationship between these different types of learning and what is often referred to as the attainment of conceptual understanding.

The focus of the chapter is on explaining the types of learning, rather than the specific techniques involved in teaching each of these.

Discriminations

Discriminations are an integral part of the learning of virtually all academic skills. Consider, for example, what is involved in learning numerals. The teacher may say to the student 'point to the five' when displaying a set of numbers. The appropriate student behaviour is, of course, to point to 5 if the number is present. That is, the student must identify the numeral. Later, the teacher may point to a 5 and ask the student to name the number. The required student behaviour is to say 'five'. Both of these behaviours, identification and naming, are types of discriminations. The common aspect of all discriminations is that there are a number of possible alternative responses, each of which is associated with a particular stimulus. The exact nature of the response is defined by the problem. For example, in an identification task the specified response may be pointing. The student has available a number of alternative responses (pointing at 1 or 2 or 3, etc.), each associated with a particular numeral (1, 2, 3, etc.). Similarly, in a naming task, the response is to say the number word. A number of alternatives again exist (saying 'one' or 'two' or 'three', etc.). Students are considered to have mastered the discrimination when they consistently choose the appropriate response for that particular stimulus or set of stimuli.

Discriminations vary in difficulty, with several factors determining the ease of discrimination. One such factor is the number of alternatives from which the student has to choose. For example, a common procedure for teaching identification of numerals is to begin with the group 1 to 5. This means that there are only four incorrect alternatives for each correct alternative; for example, for 3 the incorrect alternatives are 1, 2, 4 and 5. (A correct alternative is sometimes denoted by the symbol **S+**, and an incorrect alternative by **S−**). Typically, mastery of this group of numerals will lead to the student being taught an expanded group of numerals and exposed, therefore, to a larger set of incorrect alternatives (or S–s). A second factor influencing discrimination difficulty is the difference between the S+ and each S–. For example, students often have considerable difficulty in learning to discriminate 6 from 9, because of their physical similarity. In contrast, discriminating 6 from 1 is not such a difficult task because the two are not so similar.

ATTENTION

What is involved in learning a discrimination? It is generally considered that it involves two main processes (House, 1982; Trabasso & Bower, 1968), one of which is attention. To succeed at a discrimination, the student must attend to the relevant **dimension** in that task. Stimulus materials typically vary in many dimensions. For example, a particular instance of the numeral 3 has a certain colour, size, and is written on a surface of particular texture. These attributes of the stimulus are commonly called dimensions. However, the only thing that is relevant for identifying it as the numeral 3 is its shape or form. In other words, form is the relevant dimension to which the student must attend, and all other dimensions (i.e., colour, size, etc.) are irrelevant. Table 1.1 gives some examples of dimensions, and possible values within those dimensions.

Table 1.1

Dimension	Examples of values
size	large, small
colour	green, brown
form	square, round, '3', 'a'
texture	rough, smooth
novelty	familiar, unfamiliar
position	left, in front of
speed	slow, fast

In any discrimination, there will be at least one relevant dimension and a number of irrelevant dimensions. Take, for example, the case of a student learning to identify colours. Different stimuli (e.g., banana, flower, clothing) may vary in terms of size, form, texture and so forth, but may all have the same colour (i.e., yellow). Identification of colours requires the student to attend to the relevant dimension of colour, and ignore the other irrelevant dimensions that are present. Only then can the student be expected to learn the discrimination. Indeed, a major challenge in any discrimination learning situation is to direct the student's attention to the relevant dimension.

Attention to the relevant dimension does not mean that the student has learned the discrimination. As indicated earlier, there is another important component to discrimination learning. This involves the student learning to respond to S+s and S–s according to their values on the relevant dimension. For example, identifying numerals requires the student first to attend to form and then to learn to identify the particular form that characterizes each numeral. Seldom, however, are all instances of a stimulus exactly the same in terms of the relevant dimension. For example, the form of any given numeral is also likely to vary; thus, 'three' can be written as 3 or 3. Similarly, a letter may appear in any of a variety of typescripts. The various instances of a particular stimulus comprise what can be called a **stimulus class**. Part of the student's task is to learn that all members of this class are equivalent. For this learning to occur, students must be presented with a number of examples of each stimulus, with these examples differing in terms of the relevant dimension. For example, a number of instances of the letter '*b*' written in different typescripts should be presented if the student is to learn the stimulus class '*b*'. Similarly, various hues of yellow must be presented if the student is to learn the stimulus class 'yellow'. As we shall see in the next section, establishing relations between different stimulus classes is in itself an important part of many basic learning activities.

In summary, then, discriminations involve choosing the correct alternative from a number of incorrect ones. The difficulty of doing this is influenced by the number of incorrect alternatives and their similarity to the correct one. The processes involved in discrimination learning are first to attend to the relevant dimension or dimensions and then to respond appropriately to the correct and incorrect alternatives. The behaviour required in responding varies between tasks, but identification and naming are common examples at the basic level. The alternatives themselves may vary in a number of ways; the variants comprising a particular alternative (e.g., all triangles) are described as a stimulus class.

Relations

Many simple learning tasks involve the forming of relations between different stimulus classes. This can be illustrated by considering the activity of reading. One of the requirements of the reading process is the immediate recognition of a certain repertoire of words. Essentially, this involves the establishment of relations between the printed word and the verbal form of the word. If a student sees the word 'the' and says the word, or a child is able to identify the word 'the' having heard the verbal form of the word, the relations between the printed and verbal forms of the word have been established.

Let us now consider a more detailed example — spelling out all possible relations. Using the number 5 as an example, it is possible to identify four different stimulus classes which the child needs to learn: (**1**) the numeral 5, (**2**) the written word five, (**3**) the spoken word 'five' and (**4**) the set ∴. Table 1.2 shows all twelve possible relations among these four stimulus classes. Fortunately, it is not necessary for the student to learn all of these relations (Sidman & Tailby, 1982). In fact, it is only necessary to learn six of these twelve relations, because a relation learned in one direction will automatically exist in the other direction. For example, a student who learns to say 'five' when he or she reads the word five should be able to identify the word five on hearing it spoken. Similarly, a student who learns to write the numeral when presented with the set ∴ should be able to identify a set of 5 when given the numeral.

Even so, it would seem that there is still a very large number of relations to be taught, even at the most fundamental level. The instructor would appear to be faced with a formidable task in teaching all these relations. Fortunately, however, further economies are achieved because many of these relations are learned although they are not actively taught. Let us consider the example of a common noun, such as dog. Here there are three main stimulus classes: the visual

Table 1.2

	numeral	word	spoken	set
numeral		5 — five	5 — 'five'	5 — ⁙
word	five — 5		five — 'five'	five — ⁙
spoken	'five' — 5	'five' — five		'five' — ⁙
set	⁙ — 5	⁙ — five	⁙ — 'five'	

form (e.g., dogs or pictures of dogs), the spoken form 'dog', and the written word *dog*. As suggested by the preceding discussion, the instructor's aim is for the student to regard each of these as equivalent. This means that the student must learn the three possible relations between these classes. These relations are visual-spoken, written-visual and spoken-written. In fact, however, it is only necessary to ensure that the student has learnt two of these relations. When this has occurred, the third will follow automatically. Students would normally learn the correspondence between the visual and spoken form first. If they then learn the correspondence between the written and visual forms, they would automatically acquire the spoken-written correspondence. Similarly, if they learn the spoken-written correspondence after the visual-spoken form, they would automatically acquire the written-visual correspondence. Once all possible relations are acquired, the student has learned what is known as an **equivalence class**.

Returning to the example of the number 5, it will be remembered that we identified four stimulus classes and six relations for the student to learn. The six relations are shown in each of the two examples in Table 1.3. Now, if the student learns the first three relations in either example, the second three relations will automatically be acquired. At this stage the student has acquired the equivalence class for the number 5. In other words, the instructor's task can be somewhat less daunting than initially appeared to be the case.

Table 1.3

	Example 1	*Example 2*
Learned	'five' — 5	'five' — 5
	'five' — five	'five' — ⚄
	'five' — ⚄	5 — five
Automatic	5 — five	'five' — five
	5 — ⚄	5 — ⚄
	five — ⚄	five — ⚄

This has important implications for instructors. Efficient instruction will depend on their doing three things. Firstly, they must recognize all possible relations. Secondly, they must identify those relations already learned by the student. And thirdly, they must identify the relations to be taught, so that the equivalence class is taught in the most economical manner.

Rules

When students have mastered some discriminations and learned a set of relations, they are in a position to advance further via yet another type of learning. Perhaps the major way in which this can occur is through the learning of what are known as procedures and rules. In essence, this involves learning the sequence of steps which must be carried out in order to demonstrate a particular skill or to solve a problem.

Let us illustrate what we mean by considering a couple of rules of different complexity. An example of a very simple rule is the elementary procedure a student follows when counting from one number to the next. In this activity, saying one number provides a cue for the next number in the sequence. That is, in learning to count, the student is actually learning a set of simple rules of the form:

Cue Number	Next Number
1 ⟶	2
2 ⟶	3
3 ⟶	4
4 ⟶	5

etc.

Counting involves combining these elementary rules into an integrated sequence.

At a more complex level, the rule may involve a number of steps. For example, certain addition problems (e.g., 28 + 16) require a series of single-digit additions. However, in order to solve such a problem the student also has to learn the new rule of 'carrying'. How students actually learn such rules will be examined in Chapter 4.

Rules are an integral part of academic performance in all skill domains, although in some areas such as spelling and grammar they cannot be as universally applied as they can in mathematics. For example, students learn that writing the plural form of a noun involves the addition of an 's' to the singular form. But they also have to learn that there are many exceptions to this rule, the most notable being the case of words ending in 'y'. Consequently, they learn that a second rule is appropriate; namely, substituting 'ies' for the 'y'.

When the execution of some skills is examined, it becomes apparent that there are also different levels of rules. More complex academic skills involve higher-order rules which may be learned only after certain lower-order rules have been applied. For example, if a student is to understand multiplication rules, he or she must first learn the rules of addition. The addition rules can be regarded, therefore, as prerequisites for the multiplication rules. In any area of learning it is possible to identify the prerequisite structures which show how rules at one level are dependent on lower-level rules. This means, of course, that a major component in the acquisition of more sophisticated skills is the continuing expansion of the student's repertoire of rules.

Production Skills

What is meant by 'production' skills? Most academic skills require the production, or physical performance, of some form of behaviour. Writing and speaking are the most common examples. Learning of these skills differs from other types of learning. With most aspects of academic learning, correctness is judged in an all-or-none fashion. For example, in response to the question 'how much is 5 + 7?', '13' is close to the answer of '12', but it is no more correct than is '15'. This applies to many other skills, like spelling and word identification. The major difference between production skills and these other aspects of academic learning is that, for production skills, correctness is not judged in this all-or-none fashion.

For example, a student learns to write the letters of the alphabet over a long period of time, and only gradually reaches the stage of competent letter formation. The student may know the procedure for producing (or writing) a particular letter at an early stage. However, accurate production of that letter may improve slowly over an extended period of time. During this process, the letters that the student produces could not be judged to be right or wrong, but rather as attempts at reproducing the desired form. It is quite possible that any letter could be judged to be closer or further away from this desired form than any other. In these cases, judgement of the behaviour is relative rather than all-or-none.

Most physical or motor skills fall into this category of being gradually and imperfectly acquired. Running, throwing a ball and riding a bicycle are all learned in a gradual fashion. It is only with experience that the behaviour gradually comes close to the desired form. Other skills of this nature include articulation of letter sounds, their combination into whole words, and writing, as mentioned above. In each case, the procedures may be known, but truly effective production is only gradually acquired.

In some cases of basic academic learning the central focus is the production skill itself. Perhaps the best example of this is handwriting. In others, the production skill is usually learned well in advance of the academic learning that exploits it. For example, students usually learn to articulate numbers prior to using them as answers to mathematical problems.

Production skills are generally learned by a process known as **shaping**. That is, the student learns by making successive attempts to reproduce the desired form. Initial attempts may be relatively poor, but over time they may approach this target. Later, in Chapter 4, the various methods of designing instruction suited to developing production skills will be discussed.

Conceptual Understanding

Finally, before moving on to consideration of instructional principles, it is appropriate to comment at least briefly on the interrelationships between the types of learning outlined in this chapter and what is involved in a student achieving what is usually called 'conceptual understanding'. It is often noted that there is a difference between a student being able to perform a certain academic skill and having the proper conceptual grasp. For example, a student could learn that $2 + 2 = 4$. At any time that such a problem arose, the student could give the correct answer. However, for the student to have a conceptual grasp of this arithmetical statement, there are a number of prerequisites that he or she needs to have learned. The student needs to have learned addition through some type of counting rule (e.g., if counting in 1s only, the student starts at 2, counts to 3 and then to 4; if counting in 2s, then only one step is necessary). In turn, the student must have learned the general procedure for counting from a given number (by 1s only, or by 2s, or 5s, etc.). This must be preceded by learning numeral:set relations, and this by the identification of numerals and sets.

Let us take another example. A student may learn to write and, through successive approximations, produce accurate letters and words. But even at a basic level of writing single letters and words, conceptual understanding requires a knowledge of spoken-written relations as well as identification of sounds and of letters and words. Without these, the student is simply going through a mechanical task.

In any area, then, the student can only be said to have conceptual understanding when the whole chain of prerequisites has been learned. This also means that if the prerequisite elementary levels (e.g., basic relations and rules) are not learned properly, then conceptual understanding is unlikely to be achieved.

Chapter 1   Exercises
Try the following exercises. When you have completed them, check the answers at the end of the book.

1.   For each of the discriminations listed below, identify —
   (a)   the relevant dimension or dimensions
   (b)   some of the irrelevant dimensions which could be used in teaching
   (c)   the values of correct (S+) and incorrect (S–) alternatives on the relevant dimension:
      (i)   a triangle

      (ii)   the spoken letter 's'

      (iii) the word 'the'.

2.   For the common noun **computer**, specify —
   - **(a)** the major stimulus classes
   - **(b)** all possible relations between these classes
   - **(c)** the minimum number of relations which must be taught if the student is to learn the equivalence class
   - **(d)** the likely order in which these relations would be taught.

3.   Specify the rules used in written English language for the following:
   - **(a)** demarcation of the beginning and end of a sentence
   - **(b)** the most common method of modifying adjectives to make comparisons between two things and between three or more things — for example, modifying the adjective 'slow' to compare two trains, and three or more trains
   - **(c)** the simplest procedure for joining two simple sentences.

4.   Specify a rule to solve single-digit addition problems.
   (For examples of more complex rules, see exercises in Chapter 4.)

5.   Identify the production skills and the rules associated with performing the following tasks:
   - (i)   counting aloud by units to 10
   - (ii) saying aloud the plurals of words such as ball, hat, dog
   - (iii) typing one's own name on a keyboard.

Chapter 2
General instructional principles: part 1

In Chapter 1 the different types of learning involved in the acquisition of basic academic skills were discussed. Chapters 2, 3 and 4 describe the methods by which each of these types of learning can be achieved. There is no doubt that the efficiency of students' learning is critically dependent on the method adopted. It is necessary to elaborate those principles of instruction which when implemented appropriately **(a)** enable all students to learn, **(b)** lead to efficient learning, and **(c)** will produce what was referred to earlier as conceptual understanding. Obviously these are ambitious goals, but they can be achieved if instruction is carefully planned.

A person in a teaching role who wishes to achieve these goals needs to understand the principles and to master the techniques associated with each of these methods. There are three key elements to the design of any instructional program. First, a requirement of any learning is that the student receives some sort of **feedback**. Second, before students progress they should demonstrate **mastery** of, or competence with the material already covered. These issues are dealt with in this chapter. Finally, instruction should be organized so that the student progresses gradually from an initial relatively easy level through increasingly more difficult levels. This provides an opportunity for students to receive positive feedback as they progress. Chapters 3 and 4 deal with this important aspect of instruction.

Feedback

Most instructors have some understanding of the role of feedback and use it as a matter of course. However, research shows that both the type of feedback and the exact manner in which it is used are of critical importance (Adams, 1976; Bandura, 1969). If instruction is to be effective, therefore, these principles must be taken into account. The next section will describe how this can be done.

ROLE OF FEEDBACK

It is generally agreed that feedback has two basic roles. One is a corrective or instructional role, and the other is a motivational one. Most forms of feedback perform both functions. Each of these will be discussed in turn.

Instructional

The most elementary form of instructional feedback is information on whether the student is right or wrong. The instructor might provide this information by simply telling the student or marking the work with a tick or cross. In other situations, however, there is not such a neat dichotomy between right and wrong. For example, certain activities (e.g., an essay) may not be able to be broken down into discrete units and consequently need to be judged using a scale more complex than a simple right–wrong dichotomy. A typical example might be a 10-point marking scale. Other feedback may be even more complex and less precise in nature: for example, in judging written expression two pieces of work may be judged to be of different quality even though both may be grammatically correct.

Any form of feedback which simply rates correctness or quality has limited informational value for the student. If students' work can be judged as simply right or wrong, that information could be enhanced by indicating the correct answer. Where correctness can only be judged imprecisely, an ideal form of an answer could be provided. However, there is considerable research to show that an even better method is to highlight the differences between the students' work and the ideal piece of work (Welford, 1976). In some cases it may also be necessary to show how the ideal form is produced. In handwriting, for example, the best form of feedback is to show the student the model letter, and then draw the student's attention to the differences between that ideal and his or her own letter. It may also be necessary to show how the model is produced. There are many other examples of this process. In evaluating an essay, the instructor can indicate to the student exactly how the essay could be improved, together with an example of relevant sections of an ideal essay. In elementary maths, the student who answers that 2 + 2 = 3 should be told the correct answer and shown the difference between the two answers. The student should also be given further instruction on how to solve this problem. Typically, this would involve an abbreviated form of the initial instruction provided.

To summarize then, the best instructional feedback has several key elements: **(1)** some indication as to the correctness of the student's answer, **(2)** provision of an ideal answer, **(3)** drawing the student's attention to the differences between the answer given and the ideal solution, and optionally **(4)** extra instruction on how such an ideal could be produced. In incorporating these features, care should always be taken to avoid making feedback too complex for the student to comprehend or to remember. Each of the steps above requires a certain amount of effort on the part of the teacher or instructor. Some might question the value of this effort. Clearly, it may be difficult to implement such extensive feedback in practice, particularly in classroom or other large group situations. However, it can be argued that the priority is to provide quality feedback. This may sometimes mean that the number of problems or tasks attempted by the student and evaluated by the instructor will be less. A second question that may be raised concerns the provision of an ideal answer. It could be argued that for many tasks there is no single ideal. Under such circumstances, one compromise may be for the instructor to provide a range of ideals rather than attempting to provide a single one. For example, several different ways of expressing the same idea may be suggested to a student in preference to the form used by the student.

Motivational

The other role of feedback is motivational in nature. In fact corrective feedback itself has motivating properties. For example, simply telling students that they are right can be a powerful reinforcer; in other words, students are more likely to answer such problems in the same way in the future. In contrast, telling students that they are wrong may have the opposite effect. In this case, students may be less likely to answer in the same manner in the future.

There is an additional form of motivation which can come into play. If students are consistently correct, then they are able to progress to new and possibly more complex material. For example, as students' reading skills (e.g., vocabulary, comprehension) improve, they can progress to reading more challenging and interesting books.

By themselves, the immediate feedback and the opportunity to progress may be sufficient motivation for the student. Many students want to get everything right; for them, making a mistake is something to be avoided. Many students are also strongly reinforced by progression to advanced learning. The term self-motivated (Harter, 1983; White, 1959) is often used to describe such students.

There are instances where corrective feedback and the opportunity to progress may not be sufficiently motivating. This may arise with particular groups of students or when the tasks involved are especially demanding. In these cases it is necessary to find alternative or additional **reinforcers** for correct performance. These reinforcers need to be selected carefully and used in an appropriate manner.

A fundamental principle in the choice of reinforcers — but one which is frequently ignored — is that the reinforcer must be appropriate for the individual (Alberto & Troutman, 1986). What is reinforcing for one child need not be for another. Factors such as age and personal interests will all be determinants of what is reinforcing for the individual.

One form of **reinforcement** which is available in almost any teaching situation and effective with most individuals is **social reinforcement**. Examples of social reinforcers include attention directed to the student by the instructor, communication of approval through facial expressions and gestures, and praise.

A second form of reinforcement which is of general utility is access to favourite activities. For example, with a student who prefers reading to maths, the learning situation may be arranged to provide the student with the opportunity to read if his or her maths work is satisfactorily completed. Alternatively, the reinforcer may be free time for the student to engage in activities of his or her choice.

One problem arises when an instructor is dealing with a group of individuals. Reinforcer selection may be based on the age and other characteristics of the group, but there will also be individual differences. For example, not all eight-year-olds find the same activities reinforcing or respond in the same way to social reinforcement. Consequently, the instructor may only gradually identify appropriate reinforcers for each individual. An alternative solution to this problem is to provide students with a choice of reinforcers. As mentioned previously, students may be given a period of time to engage in a chosen activity: one student may read, one may draw and one may play on a computer.

There are various ways of identifying the effective reinforcers for an individual. For example, the student may be asked what activities he or she likes doing most. The same information may be obtained by observing the student. Does the student spend his or her free time in certain solitary pursuits or seeking the attention of and interacting with others? While these methods will help identify potential reinforcers, the ultimate test is to try them. Thus, for example, if a student appeared not to respond to praise given consistently, then praise is obviously not reinforcing for that individual and the instructor must seek an alternative.

One other important consideration in choosing a reinforcer is its magnitude; that is, do you give a little or a lot of praise, do you allow the student to engage in a desired activity for a short or long period, and so on? In making this decision, there are two important factors that must be balanced. One is that larger reinforcers are generally more effective; the other is that the larger the reinforcer, the more rapidly it will lose its effectiveness with repeated use (Martin & Pear, 1983). Thus, it is necessary to use a reinforcer that is large enough to be effective, but not so large that it loses its effectiveness after only a few occasions.

There are two objections that are sometimes raised to the use of reinforcement. Some argue that students may come to learn only when those reinforcers are available. The alternative is to rely on the natural reinforcers (e.g., achievement) present in the situation. However, there are situations in which, and students for whom, the natural reinforcers are not effective. In such situations, the instructor who desires to use only natural reinforcers must consider the need to ensure that learning occurs. It can be argued that the best solution is to use whatever reinforcers are necessary to ensure that efficient learning occurs and then to reduce the dependence on the reinforcer gradually. Techniques for doing this are described in the next section.

The other objection is that the use of reinforcement in this way promotes undesirable competition between students. Those who raise this issue are concerned that low-achieving students will secure little reinforcement compared to their high-achieving peers. This objection arises from a failure to appreciate that the effects of reinforcement are dependent upon the way in which it is given. In most academic situations, reinforcement should be dependent on the student progressing beyond what that student has achieved before. How the student's performance relates to that of other students is not at issue. In other words, individual improvement should be the criterion for reinforcement rather than relative merit.

USING FEEDBACK

Thus far, the various forms of feedback have been considered. Turning to the issue of how feedback might best be implemented, the way in which this is done depends very much on the stage of learning that the individual has reached. Most learning situations involve two broad stages. In the initial or acquisition stage, the material being presented and/or the demands placed on the student may be made progressively more difficult until the target level is reached. In the second stage, this newly acquired behaviour has to be performed consistently. For example, when learning to draw a circle, the acquisition stage may begin with the student being shown a model of the required behaviour and physically guided in its execution. Gradually these aids may be withdrawn, with the student being required to produce progressively more accurate circles. Eventually the student will reach a stage where acceptable circles are being produced in the absence of supporting cues. At this point he or she is about to make the transition to the second stage where the new behaviour is consolidated as a result of further practice.

In the acquisition stage, corrective feedback and additional reinforcement should be fully exploited. If the corrective feedback is sufficiently motivating, this alone may suffice. However, if this is not the case, additional reinforcement should be used. The feedback and additional reinforcement serve both to guide the student and to motivate the student as the requirements become more demanding.

At this stage, whatever feedback is used should be given frequently and without undue delay. By ensuring that the delay is not too long, the student is better able to compare his or her work with the correct or ideal outcome and to act on this feedback before any further errors are made. Providing feedback in this way may sometimes present practical difficulties, but the trade-off is that learning will be more efficient.

In the second stage of learning, the student practises this newly acquired behaviour. It is during this stage that the student's reliance on whatever forms of feedback have been provided should be reduced. In achieving this, it is important that the withdrawal of feedback be gradual rather than abrupt. Abrupt withdrawal of feedback may produce a regression in performance (Kazdin, 1984; Ross, 1978).

The first component of feedback to be withdrawn should be any additional reinforcement that may have been provided. The withdrawal process should be irregular as well as gradual. That is, with corrective feedback unchanged, the additional reinforcement should be presented less and less frequently and in an unpredictable manner. Eventually, it will only be necessary to provide additional reinforcement occasionally.

The following example illustrates this process. A student's answers to maths questions are checked after each problem and correct answers are reinforced with praise (e.g., 'very good', 'you got that one right'). Once the stage of simply practising a certain type of problem has been reached, the instructor, while still indicating whether the answer is right or wrong, may change the form of the praise (e.g., 'you are doing very well') and use it, on average, every second, then third, then fifth correct answer. The timing of this additional reinforcement should be such that the student never knows which problem it will follow. Eventually praise may be given only at the end of a work period. With very large groups, of course, the overall frequency of reinforcement may have to be reduced from this ideal.

The process of using and then gradually withdrawing reinforcement serves another important function. Earlier it was pointed out that some individuals are not sufficiently motivated by corrective feedback and the opportunity to progress. It was argued that additional reinforcers should be used in such cases. When this occurs, the corrective feedback becomes associated with the additional reinforcement. This association results in the feedback itself acquiring greater motivating value (O'Leary & O'Leary, 1977). For example, associating praise with being told that one is right may make the latter a more powerful reinforcer. It may then be possible to withdraw the additional reinforcement gradually, leaving the feedback to maintain the behaviour.

Having withdrawn any additional reinforcement, the student's dependence on the instructor can be further reduced by the gradual withdrawal of corrective feedback. This process can be carried out in a manner similar to that described for additional reinforcement. That is, corrective feedback can be given for two problems at the same time, then three and so forth. Eventually a student may be able to do a set amount of work (e.g., a series of addition problems, writing a line of letters), only receiving corrective feedback at the end. However, if it is found that performance is deteriorating during such a progression, then it may be necessary to return temporarily to more frequent corrective feedback.

One other approach to reducing reliance on instructor feedback is to teach the student to monitor his or her own performance (Rosenbaum & Drabman, 1979), a process known as **self-monitoring**. This requires that the student has available a correct answer (e.g., the correct answer to a maths problem, an ideal version of a letter that the student is learning to draw) which he or she can compare to his or her own version. A further form of performance monitoring involves the student self-checking the various steps involved in executing the task. In Chapter 4 will be found an outline of how a student learns a step-by-step approach to learning complex skills.

During this second stage, another goal of the instructor should be that the student can perform the behaviour independently of the context. The term **generalization** is used to describe this phenomenon. A person is said to show generalization when he or she exhibits a behaviour outside the context in which it was learned. Ensuring that generalization occurs requires that the instructor varies both the manner and the context in which the material is presented (Stokes & Baer, 1977). For example, when teaching students that $2 + 2 = 4$, the problem initially may be written on the board in a horizontal arrangement. Once students have mastered this, it may then be presented in a vertical arrangement, written on paper and using a variety of concrete examples. In this way the student learns to solve the problem independent of context.

The instructor does not, however, need to present the problem in every possible context; it is only necessary to present a reasonable variety of examples. It is best to progress from examples that are minimally different from the original to increasingly more different examples. Very different examples presented at an early stage may be too difficult for the student. Sometimes generalization may be further encouraged if problems or examples are presented in different situations. This may involve, for example, a different instructor (e.g., a parent or a different teacher) or a different physical location.

The process of self-monitoring referred to above (p.21) may make generalization easier (Belmont, Butterfield & Ferretti, 1982; Glynn, Thomas & Shee, 1973). A student engaging in self-monitoring is automatically less reliant on the instructor and is, therefore, in a better position to practise the behaviour in a variety of contexts.

In summary, feedback is used differently at different stages of learning. In the acquisition stage, as much instructional and motivational feedback as is necessary is used. Subsequently, the newly acquired behaviour is practised, with the feedback becoming less frequent. Normally, the motivational feedback is withdrawn first. At this stage the task should also be varied to promote generalization. If the student can monitor his or her own performance, then both the withdrawal of feedback and generalization is made easier.

Mastery

At the outset of this chapter it was stated that there are three key elements to the design of any instructional program. One of these, feedback, has just been discussed. Attention may now turn to the second of these, mastery. It is a key requirement of effective learning that student progression be contingent upon mastery of more basic levels (Gagné, Briggs & Wager, 1988). There are two things that the instructor must do in order for mastery learning to occur. One is the precise specification of what the student is to learn. The second is allowing students to progress at their own rate, regardless of time taken or how their performance compares with others. Each of these will be discussed in turn.

OBJECTIVES

Consider what is meant by precise specification of learning objectives. It is essential that the objective be clear and concrete and that the student's performance be directly comparable with it. In some cases, statements of objectives may be very easy to produce. For example, when learning the alphabet, the objective(s) may be that the student **(1)** correctly names any letter presented, **(2)** selects a named letter from an array of letters, irrespective of factors such as typescript, writing material, etc. In other cases, specifying the objectives may be more difficult.

Consider a problem previously discussed in Chapter 1: teaching students so that they might attain a conceptual grasp of single-digit addition problems such as $2 + 3 = 5$. As an objective, this is neither concrete, nor does it lend itself easily to evaluation. However, as shown in Chapter 1, it is possible to specify a chain of prerequisites that, once learned, result in conceptual understanding. Each of these prerequisites can be specified in terms which are concrete and allow evaluation. For example, one of the specified prerequisites is that students learn the general procedure of counting from a given number. In this case, the objective can be stated as follows: beginning from any number in the range 1 to 9, the student can count by ones up to 10. The other prerequisites for understanding such an addition problem, and possible objectives, are shown in Table 2.1 (for simplicity, a particular method of teaching addition is assumed).

Table 2.1

Prerequisite	Objectives
Identification of numerals	— can name any numeral 1–10
	— can select specified numeral from array of numerals
Identification of sets	— can match sets with equal numbers of elements
	— can compose a set of specified numbers
Numeral: Set relations	— can match a set to the appropriate numeral
	— can match a numeral to the appropriate set

Counting by ones from a given number	—	beginning from any number in the range 1–9, can count by ones up to 10
A counting rule for addition	—	in response to + sign, begins counting from the numeral preceding the sign by a number of units equal to the numeral following the sign.

Consider a very different case, but one in which it is also difficult to specify the objectives — a child's essay. Depending on the instructor's objectives and the child's level of development, criteria such as the following may be used to generate mastery aims or objectives: correct spelling, grammar and punctuation; appropriate vocabulary level and semantic complexity; logical consistency; coherent story line, theme or subject matter.

These criteria can be used to produce precise objectives appropriate for the student level. For example, one of the objectives for punctuation may specify that students begin sentences with an upper case letter and end them with a full stop. In some cases it may be much more difficult to produce precise objectives. For example, appropriate semantic complexity or vocabulary level are difficult to specify without the use of psychometric instruments. (Those interested in this more precise form of measurement should consult texts such as Anastasi (1990), Salvia & Ysseldyke (1981) and Sattler (1982).) Nevertheless, the instructor will have some notion of an appropriate target level. The problem, however, is to translate such notions into a more objective form. One of the main ways in which this could be done is by using sample essays that exhibit the appropriate characteristics (written by the instructor, or obtained from prior students or story books). These may be compared to the students' work in terms of semantic complexity or vocabulary level.

It should be clear from these examples that there are two steps in producing precise mastery objectives. One step involves dividing the task into elements. In some cases the elements will be clearly identifiable components of the task; for example, some obvious elements of addition problems are setting out the problem properly, adding the units column, etc. Other elements may not be simple components of the task. In the addition example, neatness is one such element. Other examples are provided by the essay problem described above. Here the elements are spelling, grammar, punctuation, etc.

The other step involves what might be called **operationalizing** each element. This involves stating each objective in terms of the actual behaviour required of the student. In other words, operationalizing each element requires the instructor to specify what students must do in order to demonstate that they have met that objective. For example, students may well comprehend a passage that they have read. But in order to demonstrate reading comprehension, they might be required to summarize the passage accurately and to answer questions of an appropriate level of difficulty.

It is often very difficult to specify mastery objectives. The following example illustrates how one might go about this. For this illustration, learning the concept of number will be considered. The first stage is for the instructor to work out his or her own notion of what the concept of number entails. Some of the questions that he or she might ask include the following:

— What are some of the common conceptions of number?
— How does someone manifest knowledge of the concept of number?
— What would a person do to show that he or she is different from someone who does not have the concept of number?

and
— Are these all the things that the person needs to be able to do?

The aim of this exercise is to produce a list of behaviours which characterize someone who understands the concept of number. The next stage involves independent validation of this list of behaviours to ensure that what the instructor proposes to evaluate accurately reflects the concept of number. The way in which this is done can vary. A simple procedure would be to consult expert sources such as mathematics books, and to ask other instructors and people considered to have some expertise in this area to evaluate whether or not each of these behaviours reflects knowledge of the concept of number. More elaborate validation procedures would involve testing students and determining whether the list of behaviours is able to differentiate between students with different levels of conceptual understanding of number. While such procedures may involve some effort, they will provide information that will improve the set of objectives. A detailed discussion of validation procedures may be found in Anastasi (1990).

PACING

The other key aspect of mastery learning is that students should be allowed to progress at their own rate. The virtues of self-pacing in comparison with conventional teaching methods have been well documented (Block & Burns, 1977; Hyman & Cohen, 1979). Under this form of instruction, the important thing is not how the student's progress compares with his or her peers, but rather how the student is progressing in relation to a series of target objectives. By having a graded series of objectives, all students should be able to achieve some degree of success. Where student progress is evaluated only by comparison with the performance of peers, some students will have a very high degree of success, while others will have little.

Another problem with traditional systems is that less able students may become increasingly disadvantaged over time. This occurs when time is a criterion for progression; for example, students may move on to a new area of work after a certain time period has been spent on the earlier section, or may move to a new grade after a fixed time in an earlier grade. Where learning an earlier section may be a prerequisite for some later section, individuals who have not properly learned the earlier section will obviously have considerable difficulty. They will be learning new material, while still trying to master the old. Thus, paradoxically, students of lower ability are being set a harder task than those of higher ability.

Conventional systems may also place limitations on students of higher ability. Working under a time criterion, able students may frequently be required to continue practising a skill well beyond the achievement of mastery. This provides such students with little challenge, possibly inducing boredom and related problems.

In a system based on individual progression, what constitutes appropriate **pacing**? One of the main characteristics is the setting of an appropriate progression criterion. This has two components: specifying the objective(s) and setting the **consistency level**. The setting of objectives has already been discussed. Consistency level refers to the relative frequency with which the individual satisfies the specified objective. For example, how often a student identifies a given letter in an array of other letters, what proportion of simple addition problems a student gets right, how often a student's essay shows a consistent story line or theme. In theory, the consistency level should be set at 100%. However, given that occasional errors will always occur for a variety of reasons; in practice, consistency levels are generally set at around 90%. The exact criterion should be based upon the instructor's knowledge of what consistency of performance is required for a student to be able to tackle the next stage. Sometimes it may even be 100% consistency that is demanded. Contrast this with many conventional approaches where 50% is frequently used as the criterion. While this may seem to allow more material to be covered, students may be permitted to progress to new material with only a poor knowledge of the earlier work.

The implementation of individual pacing obviously requires monitoring of student performance. The importance of monitoring in the provision of feedback has already been discussed, and the criteria for effective monitoring are the same here.

Chapter 2   Exercises
Try the following exercises. When you have completed them, check the answers at the end of the book.

1. What might be the ideal instructional feedback given to a student in each of the following situations:
    (i)   'which one is the square?' — student is presented with a square and a triangle
    (ii) 'what is 2 + 3 ?'
    (iii) student writing the sentence 'My name is John.' and being checked for using a capital letter at the start.

2. For an instructional setting in which you have been:
    (i)   identify the reinforcers that are available
    (ii) identify the most appropriate reinforcers for at least two students.

3. For **1** (i) and **1** (ii), assume that instructor praise is to be used as motivating feedback (in addition to the instructional feedback) and describe —
    (a) the form that this motivating feedback might take
    (b) how you would identify when the transition from the acquisition stage is occurring

(c) the provision of feedback and generalization instruction in the post acquisition stage.

4. Convert the following general descriptions into mastery aims:

   (i) recognises currency

   (ii) uses punctuation (at a basic level)

   (iii) understands 'more than'

   (iv) competent classroom singing.

Chapter 3
General instructional principles: part 2

In Chapter 2 two of the key components of instructional programs — feedback and mastery learning — were reviewed. Here, the third key element of effective instruction — **structured progression** — is examined. Using structured progression, students move through gradually more difficult stages of learning in a manner that ensures success throughout. Instead of the student being presented with a set of problems and making a number of mistakes before reaching the objective, the problems are presented to ensure success from the outset. Under this system a student may begin working at a much lower level than one who is presented with problems in their final form from the outset. However, the student working under structured progression is more likely to reach the target level of competence and generally to do so more rapidly (Alberto & Troutman, 1986; Lancioni & Smeets, 1986).

The structured progression methods described here and in Chapter 4 aim to minimize the number of errors made by students. While it is often suggested that errors are essential for learning, this is not necessarily the case. What is important is that students actively choose between correct and incorrect alternatives. They are not denied exposure to incorrect alternatives, but learning is structured in such a way that they are most unlikely to choose those alternatives (Becker & Carnine, 1981; Etzel, Le Blanc, Schilmoeller & Stella, 1981). One obvious consequence of this approach is that all students — not just those of high ability — will achieve success along the way. An associated benefit is that less time and effort is put into feedback. Feedback and correction after errors is necessarily longer and more complex than after correct answers. To the extent that corrective feedback is minimized, the demands on the instructor are reduced.

There are a number of different ways of designing structured progression. A set of techniques which can be used across all types of learning (learning of discriminations, rules, etc.) — namely, **prompting** and **fading** — is described in some detail in this chapter. Other methods appropriate for particular categories of learning are presented in Chapter 4.

Prompting and Fading

One way of ensuring that a student succeeds from the outset is to provide a prompt or cue, or a set of prompts and cues, which enables the student to solve the problem. For example, a student may be provided with a detailed set of step-by-step instructions. Once the student is achieving success, these prompts can be gradually removed. This is known as fading. Thus, there is a clear progression from performing with the aid of prompts to the student performing independently. Fading is done in a manner that ensures the consistency level is high; in other words, there are relatively few errors.

PROMPTS

There are a number of different types of prompts, each of which may be used alone or in combination with others. These are described below.

Instructions

Instructions are probably the most common form of prompt, providing a means of learning by using the experience of others. Instructions normally specify a required behaviour and the conditions under which that behaviour is appropriate. For example, for a student learning addition of two 2-digit numbers with carry, one of the instructions may take the form 'when the sum of the units column is 10 or more, put the tens value in the second column'. Here the behaviour being prompted is the carrying of the tens value. The conditions under which the student should do this are when the units column adds to a number equal to or greater than ten. A different example, in the mathematics domain, might involve instructions associated with the learning of basic geometric shapes. One instruction might be 'to pick the triangle, find the shape with three points', or 'to pick the circle, find the shape with no points'. Here the prompted behaviour is to locate the one with three points or the one with no points. The appropriate conditions for producing these behaviours are being asked to pick the triangle or the circle. (Such a discrimination can, of course, be learned by other means, as will be discussed in Chapter 4.)

To provide appropriate instructions, it is necessary to identify the procedures or rules which enable the task to be done. (This is the case, even if the student is learning discriminations and relations.) Then the instructor must decide upon the form that the instruction takes — verbal or written. Verbal instructions are useful because their content can be modified as learning progresses. This flexibility is generally not available with written instructions, although computerized presentation facilitates their ongoing modification.

While we often tend to give instructions in a very abbreviated form, it is necessary to make them as explicit as possible in the very early stages of learning. Taking the example used above, the instructions for addition with carry initially should be as explicit as those given in that example. In contrast, the instruction 'add and carry' contains the elements of what the student has to do, but would only be used after the student is showing some progress.

Another consideration is whether to use external instruction or self-instruction. Self-instruction involves the student reproducing instructions that were initially provided externally. There are advantages in transferring from external to self-instruction. First, it frees the instructor for other activities such as providing feedback. More importantly, it is virtually impossible for the student to fail to attend to his or her own instructions. Self-instruction is an effective adjunct or alternative to external instruction (Meichenbaum, 1977; Whitman, 1987). It is worth noting that the development of self-instruction is sometimes encompassed under the rubric of metacognitive training.

Finally, if a student is to learn by instruction, it is necessary that he or she receives feedback after practising the behaviour. This process can be best illustrated by an example from the physical skills domain. A child wishing to play tennis may read extensively on the subject and be told by others how to do it. However, even the student who implements the instructions perfectly will probably not produce very good shots initially. Factors such as the force required, and the height of the bounce can only be learned through experience. Thus, as well as receiving instructions, the student must play shots and get feedback on them in order to learn to play well. By themselves, instructions may prompt the behaviour, and the behaviour may approximate the desired form. However, the feedback ensures that the behaviour will continue and be modified towards the final target.

Models

Another way of prompting behaviour is through the use of **models**. When people learn in this manner it is variously referred to as modelling, imitation learning or observational learning. Such learning is said to occur when a person's behaviour changes as a result of observing another's behaviour.

Modelling can be used alone or with other prompts. When used alone, it can prompt speech and body movements. Someone can imitate the vocal sounds made by another person; for example, in learning to say letters of the alphabet, or words, or in learning to sing. Similarly, observation of someone else's behaviour can serve as a means of learning the physical form of that behaviour; for example, observing someone handwriting or throwing a ball.

There are several alternative ways of using modelling in conjunction with other types of prompts. For example, it is common to combine instructions on how to do something with a demonstration of the behaviour. Thus, when teaching addition, the instructor may work through a sample problem while instructing the student in the steps involved. Another example of the combination of a model and a prompt is provided by a student learning to write. An instructor may place a model of a letter in front of the student and then physically guide the student during reproduction of the letter.

The first decision to be made when using modelling concerns the nature or form of the model. A model may involve the end result of the behaviour or the actual production of the behaviour. For example, a student might be given a model of a letter consisting solely of the completed letter. Alternatively, the letter might be drawn while the student watches. A model that consists only of the completed product does not illustrate the precise course of the behaviour to the student. It tells the student what has to be done, but not how to do it. For this reason, a model that illustrates the actual production of the behaviour is preferable in most situations, particularly in the initial stages of learning.

Where a choice has been made to use a model demonstrating the production of the behaviour, a decision then has to be made regarding the medium of presentation. This will involve choosing between a live model and one in representational form (e.g., a video, a sequence of pictures or drawings). Research has consistently demonstrated that the more realistic and life-like a model, the more effective it is likely to be (Bandura, 1969). Thus, a video of an actual person modelling a certain behaviour is likely to be more effective than a cartoon or diagram depicting the same behaviour. In turn, a real-life model will generally prove to be superior to any of these.

If a live model is used, the relationship of the person providing the model and the student becomes important (Bandura, 1971). It has been shown that the model is more likely to be effective if he or she is liked and/or respected by the student. Also, an effective model may be one that the student recognises as similar to himself or herself. Indeed, a very effective model may be a peer who is able to demonstrate the behaviour and is liked and respected by the student.

The actual behaviour of the model also determines its effectiveness (Bandura, 1971). In many cases it is necessary to exaggerate this behaviour in some manner. For example, it is often important to slow down the behaviour so that the student has the opportunity to observe it more carefully — a behaviour carried out at normal speed may be of little help. A child learning to throw a ball will not find the normal throwing action of a skilled performer very informative. In order to see the various components of shoulder, elbow, wrist action, etc.; the child would have to observe the behaviour in slow motion, and perhaps with certain aspects emphasized.

Finally, the consequences of the behaviour should be made as clear as possible. This involves the model receiving any feedback that would normally follow the behaviour (Bandura, 1969). For example, a child learning to throw a ball is more likely to model an arm action that he or she has seen result in a longer and more accurate throw. Students are more likely to adopt ways of doing things if they can see the beneficial outcomes of doing so. Thus, in the classroom students will be more likely to model recitation of number facts if the instructor has shown them how this facilitates solution of everyday maths problems.

Matching-to-sample

A prompting procedure sometimes used for teaching discriminations and relations is **matching-to-sample** (often referred to as matching). In matching-to-sample, students are presented with a sample stimulus and a range of other stimuli. They are then asked to choose from that range one which matches the sample in some given respect. For example, the student may be shown a picture of a circle and asked to find the same shape in an array of shapes that might include a circle, ellipse, square, triangle, etc. Here then the student is learning a discrimination, but the sample is serving as the prompt.

When teaching discriminations and relations, the optimal way of using matching-to-sample is by systematically varying the irrelevant dimensions so that the sample and its matching stimulus are not always exactly the same. This is illustrated by the example in Figure 3.1.

Figure 3.1

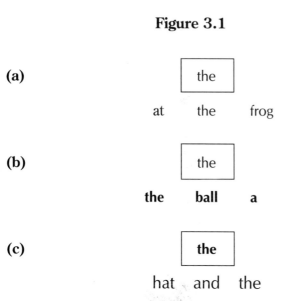

In this figure, three possible presentations from a sequence designed to teach identification of the word 'the' are shown. In presentation **(a)**, there is no difference in irrelevant dimensions between the sample and the matching stimuli. Thus, the 'the' picked out is identical to the sample. In presentation **(b)**, different S– words (i.e., incorrect alternatives) have been used and the position of 'the' has changed. In addition, the sample differs from the stimuli in terms of shading. (Another alternative is to vary colour where this is possible.) In **(c)**, the S– words are different again. The shading is different, and the sample and the stimuli also differ in size. After a number of such trials the student should be attending to the key dimension (i.e., the orthographic structure of the word) rather than any of the irrelevant dimensions.

Consider another example — the teaching of a relation between number words and sets. Figure 3.2 shows three possible presentations from a teaching sequence for this relation. Here we can see that there is variation in the types of objects used to form the sets, variation in the position of the S+ (or correct alternative), as well as variation in the size and shading of the word. A number of trials like these should result in the student attending to the dimension of numerosity.

Physical guidance

Another form of prompt simply involves the instructor physically guiding the student through the required behaviour. The main use of physical guidance is in the teaching of skills such as writing and those involved in sports and physical activities. Most commonly it will involve the manipulation of hands and arms, but also may involve other limbs or whole body guidance. It may be used alone or in conjunction with other prompts such as an instruction or a model.

Figure 3.2

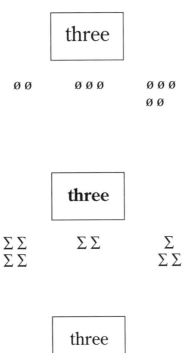

Physical guidance is particularly appropriate where stronger or more directive prompting is required. For example, a student may have difficulty copying certain aspects of ball throwing and may need to be physically guided through these actions. Similarly, the appropriate way to hold a pen may be more effectively prompted by physical guidance of the fingers than by showing the student the correct grip. Physical guidance is a very intrusive form of prompting and should only be used when necessary.

Pointers

Everyone will be familiar with the use of pointing as a prompt. While it is often used in a spontaneous manner, pointing can also be included in a well designed instructional program. The most recognizable form of pointing involves the use of the hand. However, material in a printed form or on a computer screen may use symbolic pointers, such as a picture of a pointing hand or an arrow.

Pointers are used in discrimination tasks to prompt the choice of the appropriate stimulus. For example, a student may be asked to pick out the letter '*e*' from an alphabetic list. Such a discrimination problem may be relatively difficult in the early stages of learning, and a pointing movement prior to the student's choice may function as a prompt to aid solution of the problem. Depending on the actual difficulty, the prompt may be very specific (e.g., pointing to '*e*') or more general (e.g., pointing to the section of the alphabet around '*e*').

Pointers may also be used in sequential or rule-following tasks to prompt the next step. An example of such a task is addition with carry. The first prompt might involve pointing to the units column. A second prompt could indicate the appropriate placement of the carried digit, and so forth.

Highlighting

Another form of prompting involves highlighting the stimulus in a way that attracts the student's attention. Common forms of highlighting include magnifying the size of a correct alternative, presenting the correct alternative in a different colour or shading, using different typefaces, and emphasizing phonic characteristics.

While this procedure is often used because it allows the student to perform successfully from the outset, there is an important qualification to be considered. Frequently the stimulus is modified in such a way that the student may learn to attend to an irrelevant dimension. For example, when teaching a student to discriminate between the letters H and N, the cross pieces joining the two vertical strokes may be accentuated by using a different colour for each. Under these circumstances the student may attend to colour. However, if the accentuation were to be done by bolding each to the same extent, this problem should not occur and the student should attend to letter form.

Known equivalents

Any known member of an equivalence class can be used to prompt an unknown member. In the example presented in Chapter 1 (p.6), the student who has learned to recognize the numeral 5 may learn to recognize 'five' if the numeral is used as a prompt. When a student is learning to read, a picture of an object to which the word refers may accompany the printed word. The student can identify the picture as a tree, for example, and by association eventually learns to name the word 'tree'. That is, the student is prompted by being presented with a **known equivalent** of an unknown stimulus.

At this point it is worth noting that the prompting techniques just described may also be used for corrective feedback purposes. Under such circumstances, of course, they are provided when the student makes a mistake rather than before the student responds. While the use of these techniques for feedback purposes is a legitimate one, the point to be emphasized here is that prompts can ensure that the student begins a task correctly, thereby minimizing mistakes.

FADING

In order to ensure structured progression in learning, the intensity of prompts used to aid learning must be gradually reduced. This process is known as fading. The alternative, to remove prompts abruptly, can cause marked disruption to the behaviour just established (e.g., Haupt, Van Kirk & Terraciano, 1975). For example, as described above, a picture of a tree may be used to prompt identification of the word 'tree'. If the picture is then withdrawn abruptly, the student may find it difficult to identify the word by itself. Alternatively, the picture of the tree may be made less clear over a number of trials so that there is no abrupt change. In this case, the student should make the transition to identification of the word 'tree' much more easily.

Fading should begin as soon as the student displays the behaviour reliably in the presence of the prompt(s). There are two important concerns here. First, the behaviour must be sufficiently established so that it will not be disrupted by relatively minor changes to the prompt(s). The second concern is to ensure that the student does not become too reliant on the prompt(s) as a result of continued use.

The process of fading should occur over a number of steps, each step representing a reduction in the intensity of the prompt(s). The number of steps is dictated by the ability of the student to adapt to these changes. If the student is likely to find such adaptation difficult, then there should be a greater number of small steps. On the other hand, a smaller number of large steps can be used when the student will find the transition easy. Unfortunately, there are no definitive guidelines for deciding upon the number of fading steps. An instructor's experience with the particular task and the individual student are the only guides. The steps can, however, be altered once fading has begun. Thus, by monitoring the student's performance, the steps can be changed to suit the student's rate of progression. The criterion for progressing to the next fading step should be the same as at the beginning; that is, the behaviour is reliably displayed under the particular prompt condition operating.

The end point for fading is complete independence from prompts; that is, the student reliably produces the behaviour with no assistance whatsoever. By this stage, the student's behaviour should have come under the control of the natural and appropriate cues. For example, in letter recognition, naming of the letter should be controlled by the form of the letter.

Often more than one prompt is used. Where multiple prompts have been used, fading may occur in one of two ways. Either both prompts are faded together or one may be faded before the other. Generally, the more intrusive prompt is faded first. For example, if both physical guidance and instructions were used together, physical guidance would be faded before the instructions.

Fading methods
There are five basic methods of fading a prompt:
(1) a gradual decrease in intensity of the prompt
(2) a gradual increase in the delay between the prompt and the opportunity for the student to respond to it; we will call this 'response delay'
(3) a gradual increase in the delay between the first opportunity for the student to respond and the occurrence of the prompt; we will call this 'prompt delay'
(4) a gradual abbreviation of the prompt
(5) a gradual reduction in the frequency of the prompt; that is, making it intermittent and unpredictable.

Most of these methods can be used with each type of prompt discussed in this chapter. There are, however, some exceptions. For example, while it is possible that response delay could be used with physical guidance and high-lighting, this approach is unlikely to be used in practice. In the case of physical guidance, it would mean providing some form of physical guidance but not allowing the student to carry out the behaviour until some time later.

For each type of prompt, some methods of fading are clearly superior. Let us consider each in turn.

Instructions
The most appropriate method for fading instructions is to abbreviate them by reducing the content. Take the case of a

student being instructed in how to set out a problem of two-digit addition. Initially, instruction may encompass the following statements as components:

'Write down the first number, and underneath it put the second number so that the tens column and the units column are lined up, put in a plus sign, and rule the lines for the answer underneath the second number.'

Subsequently, this instruction might be abbreviated to —

'Write down the two numbers, put in the plus sign, and rule the answer line.'

Eventually, the instruction may simply be —

'Set out the problem properly.'

Instructions may also be faded by making them more intermittent, or by the method of prompt delay (i.e., gradually allowing the student more and more time to begin to respond before any instruction is given).

Models

Reduction of intensity is one way of fading when models are used as prompts; also, the actions of a model can be abbreviated. However, in practice, the two most appropriate methods of fading a model are response delay and reducing its frequency. The former involves an increasing delay between presentation of the model and the opportunity for the student to respond. For example, an instructor teaching children to pronounce the letters *a, b, c, d* .... may first model the letter '*a*' by saying it aloud, and then getting the student to practise it. Then, the same process can be repeated for each of the other letters being learned. As the child progresses, the instructor may model groups of letters either in sequences (e.g., *a, b, c*, etc.) or in words (e.g., c a t). This necessarily imposes a delay between the modelling of a letter and the student's opportunity to say it; the longer the sequence or word, the greater will be the delay. The second method involves reducing the model's frequency. It is common for instructors to begin by using a model frequently and then, as the student progresses, the model is provided on a more occasional basis.

Matching-to-sample
In matching, fading generally involves either reducing the intensity of the sample (i.e., making it less obvious in some way) or introducing what is called delayed matching. In delayed matching there is a brief sample presentation period followed by a delay before the various stimulus alternatives are presented; this delay can be gradually increased until the sample can be eliminated without disruption.

Physical guidance
The most appropriate methods of fading physical guidance are reduction of intensity and increasing prompt delay. While there are a number of ways of combining these, one common way can be illustrated by teaching a student to hold a pen. Initially, the instructor positions the student's fingers in the appropriate manner. Then the intensity of the prompt is reduced by providing gradually more gentle assistance. Finally, the instructor's assistance is increasingly delayed, allowing the student greater opportunity to initiate the behaviour independently.

Pointers
The most common ways of fading pointers are to use the response delay and prompt delay methods. Take the case of an instructor requiring a student to pick a particular letter from an array of letters. A full prompt may be pointing to the letter and allowing the student to choose while the prompt is still present. Using response delay, the instructor points only briefly, and imposes a gradually increasing delay before the student is allowed to make his or her choice. Using prompt delay, the teacher begins by asking the student to choose, and allows time for the student to respond in the absence of

the prompt. Eventually, the student is only prompted if he or she has not responded within a reasonable period.

In some specific instances, fading the intensity of a pointer can be very useful. For example, pointers on a computer screen may be faded in exactly this way. One further method has been introduced in the earlier discussion of pointers. There an example was given where the instructor's pointing progressed from pointing directly to the required stimulus (e.g., a specific letter in an alphabetic list) to pointing to the general area of the stimulus (i.e., the section in the list in which the letter appeared).

Highlighting

With this prompt the best way of fading is to decrease intensity gradually. A perfect illustration of this is provided by the earlier example of bolding to facilitate letter discriminations. Over a series of trials the intensity of the bolding may be gradually reduced until the bolded sections can no longer be differentiated from the remaining parts of the letters.

Known equivalents

When a known equivalent of a to-be-learned stimulus is used as a prompt, the most appropriate fading methods involve reducing the intensity of that equivalent, or imposing a delay between the presentation of the equivalent and the stimulus. For example, a picture may be used to prompt selection of the referent word. Over a series of trials the picture may be made less clear (e.g., by covering it with increasingly opaque materials). Alternatively, the picture could be presented for a brief period, removed, and then, after a delay, the referent word presented.

Summary

Table 3.1 summarizes the different types of prompt available to the instructor and the methods of fading most appropriate for each.

Table 3.1

Prompt	Fading Method
instructions	abbreviation prompt delay
models	reduce frequency response delay
matching-to-sample	reduce intensity delayed matching
physical guidance	reduce intensity prompt delay
pointers	prompt delay response delay reduce intensity
highlighting	reduce intensity
known equivalents	reduce intensity prompt delay

Chapter 3   Exercises
Try the following exercises. When you have completed them, check the answers at the end of the book.

1. Provide a sequence of instructions to prompt a student in the following tasks:
    (a) using a ruler to measure the width of a pad or book
    (assume appropriate number skills)

    (b) setting out a two-digit addition problem in the form —

$$12$$
$$+\ \underline{23}$$

2. What might be the ideal way to provide a model for a student learning to place a disk into the disk-drive of a computer?

3. Describe how matching-to-sample could be used to teach identification of the colour red.

4. Describe what aspects of the stimuli you would highlight or point to when teaching the following discriminations:
    (a) discrimination of *a* from *o*
    (b) discrimination of a rectangle from a parallelogram
    (c) discrimination of next to from apart (for a pair of objects)

5. For each of the following cases, describe the most appropriate method for fading the prompt:
    (a) Question **1(a)**
    (b) Question **2**
    (c) Question **3**
    (d) Question **4(a)** using highlighting
    (e) Question **4(b)** using pointing.

Chapter 4
General instructional principles: part 3

Chapter 3 described methods of providing structured progression that are applicable to all the types of learning discussed. In this chapter, three further methods, each of which is applicable to a particular type of learning, will be discussed. First, the use of **errorless learning** procedures for teaching discriminations and relations will be considered. Second, the use of chaining for teaching rules will be described. Finally, teaching production skills by the application of shaping will be discussed.

Errorless Discrimination Learning

There are various ways of providing structured progression when teaching discriminations and relations. As indicated in Chapter 3, techniques of prompting and fading can be used. Another approach involves modifying, during the course of learning, the stimuli involved in the discrimination or relation. In errorless discrimination learning (Etzel et al., 1981; Terrace, 1963a,b) the student is initially confronted with stimuli which are easy to discriminate. The difference between these stimuli is then gradually reduced, until the student is making the required discrimination. For example, when learning to identify sets of five elements, the student may initially be asked to pick a set of five from a set of five and a set of one. Another early example may comprise a set of five and one of ten elements. Gradually, the degree of contrast is reduced until the student is ultimately required to identify a set of five contrasted with sets of six and four elements. With errorless discrimination learning, the aim is to provide examples which the student is sure to be able to solve at the beginning; progress to harder and harder examples is then contingent upon the student demonstrating success.

TECHNIQUES

There are three main ways of arranging stimuli for errorless discrimination learning (Etzel et al., 1981; Lancioni & Smeets, 1986). One has been illustrated by the example above. It involves commencing with correct (S+) and incorrect (S–) alternatives that are maximally different in terms of the relevant dimension. Gradually, the difference between the S+ and the S–s on the relevant dimension is then reduced. Let us consider another example. When teaching identification of the letter *b*, this procedure will initially involve contrasting *b* with letters such as *x*, *z* and *s*, at a later stage with letters such as *w*, *m* and *n*, and finally with letters such as *d*, *h* and *p*. There is a systematic progression from physically distinctive letters to those difficult to distinguish from *b*. If the aim is to teach the verbal-written relation simultaneously (see Chapter 1), consideration must also be given to differences in letter sound as well as shape. Thus, the letter *v*, although very different in shape, has some similarity in sound, and would not be regarded as maximally different.

The key elements of this procedure are **(a)** the S+ is constant throughout, and **(b)** over a number of trials, the S–s change from very different to very similar to S+. The similarity of S+ and S– is judged in terms of the relevant dimension for that discrimination (i.e., for letters, this is shape; for sets, this is number, etc.).

A second procedure follows a similar format, but the S– changes in intensity rather than in terms of the dimension relevant to the particular discrimination. Initially, the S+ is presented alone (i.e., S– is of zero intensity). Gradually, over a series of trials, the intensity of S– increases and it becomes more prominent. Eventually, S+ and S– are of equal intensity.

For example, a particular problem which can arise in learning the letter *b* is discrimination from its mirror-image *d*. The sequence of stimulus pairs shown below could be used in the teaching of the *b–d* discrimination.

Figure 4.1

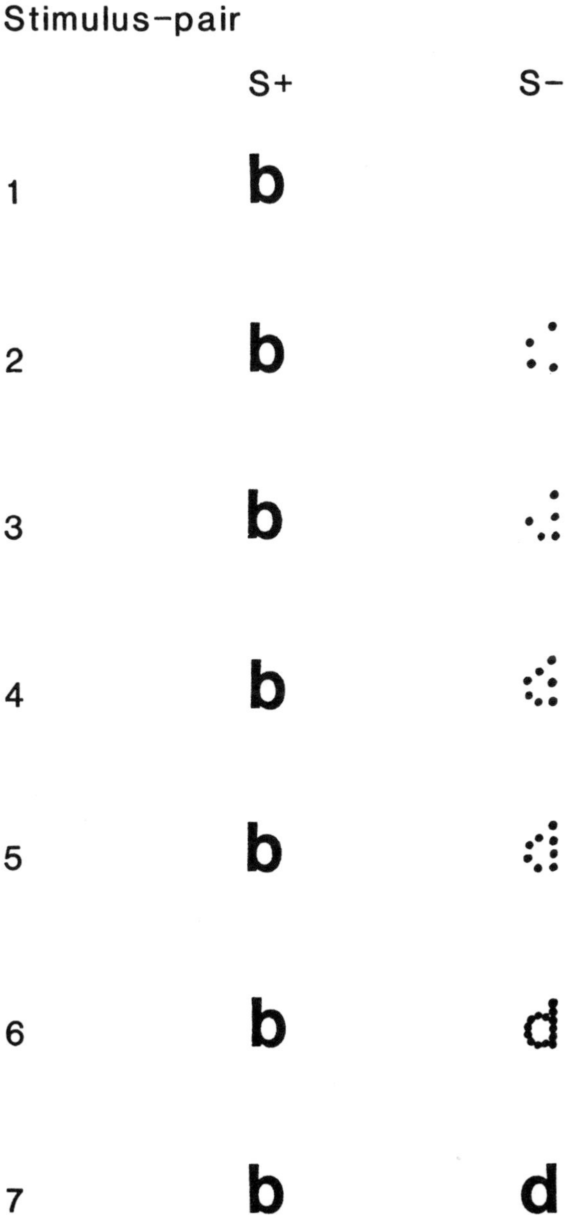

Stimulus–pair

	S+	S–
1	**b**	
2	**b**	⠢
3	**b**	⠒
4	**b**	⠲
5	**b**	⠶
6	**b**	d
7	**b**	**d**

The third procedure is appropriate when learning the discrimination requires that the student attend to shape. Consider the following example. A student has learned three basic geometric shapes: circle, square and triangle. However, he or she is now at the point where it is necessary to make finer discriminations. Thus, all rounded shapes should not be identified as circles, all four-sided shapes should not be identified as squares, etc. To begin this process, the following sequence of stimulus pairs may be used to teach the student to differentiate circles from ellipses. (The student would be asked to 'pick out the circle'.)

Figure 4.2

Stimulus-pair	S+	S–

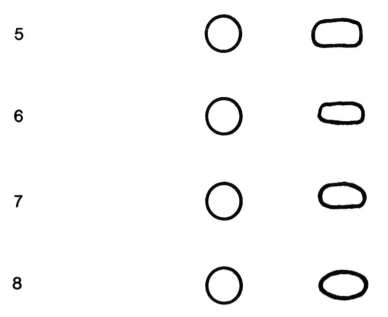

In this procedure, the initial S+/S– pair was chosen so that the contrast is one already known to, or extremely simple for, the student. Then the S– (and possibly the S+) is gradually modified into the form required in the new discrimination.

A variant of this third procedure is to begin with recognisable line-drawings which are gradually modified into S+ and S– stimuli such as letters, numerals or words. Figure 4.3 illustrates this approach with letter discriminations.

Figure 4.3   S+   S–

All these errorless learning procedures involve progression from easy to hard discriminations. The starting level of difficulty must be determined on the basis of the student's current level of performance. Thus, with the third approach it is essential that the students be familiar with and able to differentiate between the starting pictures before any modifications of the S+ and S– take place. Furthermore, the number and size of the steps should be graded according to the student's ability. That is, there should be a greater number of smaller steps for students who are likely to find the discrimination difficult. Similarly, if students are exhibiting problems with progression, the size of steps may need to be reduced and their number increased.

In general, the first of these errorless learning techniques is the preferred one. This appears to be because the student's attention is directed almost immediately to the relevant dimension (see Chapter 1). However, in many circumstances all methods are likely to be effective. It is only where the discrimination is extremely difficult for the student that clear differences between methods are likely to emerge.

Chaining

When teaching rules, **chaining** is one way of achieving structured progression (Kazdin, 1984). This approach will be illustrated with some of the more simple rules, and later its application to more complex ones will be considered. Let us begin with single-digit addition problems. As noted earlier (Chapter 2, p.25), one rule to follow when doing single-digit addition requires that, in response to a plus sign, students should begin counting from the numeral preceding the sign by a number of units equal to the numeral following the sign. This is a general counting rule for single-digit addition. The rule could be broken down into the following steps:

(1)   write down the problem in the following form $5 + 3 =$
(2)   begin counting from the first number (i.e., 5)

(3) stop counting after the number of units designated by the second number (i.e., 3)

(4) write the number reached when counting (i.e., 8) after the = sign.

What has been identified is a sequence or chain of steps that leads to the solution of single digit addition problems. Each of these steps has to be completed successfully in order to fulfil that aim. Thus, to teach a rule it is first necessary to analyse the components of the chain and, second, to provide a means by which the student can learn the chain. The process of dividing up a rule or procedure into those components is known as **task analysis** (Martin & Pear, 1983).

Once students can reliably do simple addition problems, they may progress to addition with carry. The rule for addition with carry may be task analysed as follows:

(1) set out the numbers vertically with the columns aligned, with a plus sign, and answer box

$$\begin{array}{r} 2\,7 \\ +\,1\,8 \\ \hline \end{array}$$

(2) add the numbers in the units column

$$\begin{array}{r} 2\,7 \\ +\,1\,8 \\ \hline \end{array} \quad [\,15\,]$$

(3) place the units shown in the answer box under the units and the tens value in the tens column

$$\begin{array}{r} 2\,7 \\ +\,1_{,}8 \\ \hline 5 \end{array} \quad or \quad \begin{array}{r} 1 \\ 2\,7 \\ +\,1\,8 \\ \hline 5 \end{array}$$

(4) add the numbers in the tens column and place the tens value in the answer box below the tens column

$$\begin{array}{r} 2\,7 \\ +\,1_{,}8 \\ \hline 4\,5 \end{array} \quad or \quad \begin{array}{r} 1 \\ 2\,7 \\ +\,1\,8 \\ \hline 4\,5 \end{array}$$

The components of a task analysis are rules or procedures of a lower order. For example, one component in addition with carry requires that the student perform single digit addition. The rule for this can in turn be task analysed as was shown in the earlier example. Obviously, there is no one correct way to task analyse a particular rule. Task analysis may produce a large number of lower-order components or a small number of higher-order components. Where the task is a difficult one for the student, it is appropriate to analyse the task into a large number of lower-order components. An easier task may be analysed into fewer higher-order components. One criterion that can be used for identifying the appropriate size of components is whether or not the student can do an individual component or learn it with minimal instruction. If this is not the case for any component, then that component probably requires further task analysis. For example, in the two-digit addition problem described above, a student may have difficulty with step **(3)**. If so, the step could be divided into **(a)** place the units value in the answer box under the units column, and **(b)** place the tens value in the tens column.

Learning a rule requires not only that students be able to do each of the component behaviours, but also that they perform them in the correct sequence. If this is to occur, the student has to respond to the cues which provide the information about the correct sequence. A question or statement of the problem is the initiating cue for the whole chain; for example, 'what is 27 + 18?' Within the chain itself, the cue for each component is the consequence or outcome of the previous component. In two-digit addition, therefore, the cue for component **(2)** is a problem set out in the manner shown. For component **(3)**, the cue is the answer arrived at by adding the numbers in the first column. Finally, component **(4)** is cued by having a number in the units answer box and no number in the tens answer box. (Where the sum of the units is greater than 10, there will also be a carry value in the tens column acting as a further cue.) A complete task analysis should identify these consequences or cues, as well as the component behaviours.

TECHNIQUES

There are three main ways of teaching a rule using chaining (Martin & Pear, 1983; Weiss, 1978). The first is sometimes described as **total task presentation.** With this method, the instructor helps the student through each step using appropriate prompts. Then, as the student becomes more competent, these prompts are progressively faded out. At the first attempt, the instructor may have to give considerable help so that the chain can be completed. On subsequent occasions the intrusiveness of these prompts must be reduced in accordance with the student's progress in learning the rule. In the case of addition with carry, each step may be prompted using pointing and appropriate instruction. The prompts should be designed so that the student can complete the first problem. With the next problem, the instructor may eliminate the pointing; later, the instructions may be abbreviated. At an appropriate stage, the instructions can be eliminated altogether.

In addition to the prompts, the instructor should also provide appropriate feedback both during the chain and after its completion. Initially, it may be necessary to give some feedback following each step. This feedback serves the normal instructional and motivational functions. Like the prompts, this feedback can be gradually eliminated until the student is receiving feedback only after completion of the whole chain. When this stage is reached, the natural consequences of each step will prompt the following step in the chain. Consider the addition with carry example discussed above. Here, the completed, set-out problem is the consequence of the first step which prompts the second step, the addition of numbers in the units column.

There are two alternatives to total task presentation: forward chaining and backward chaining. Both involve teaching one step at a time. With forward chaining, the student is taught the first step in the chain. Then, once competent at that, the student is asked to do the first two steps, then the first three, and so on. Teaching may be done by the use of prompting and fading with appropriate feedback. With backward chaining, the steps are also taught one at a time, but the last step in the chain is taught first. The student is then taught to do the last two steps (starting from the second last and progressing to the last), the last three (starting from the third last . . . .), and so on.

To illustrate these last two procedures, consider the example of learning single-digit addition by the following method:

Task Analysis

Step 1.   set out the problem:

$$
\begin{array}{r}
2 \\
+\,3 \\
\hline
\end{array}
$$

Step 2.   place equivalent number of dots next to each numeral:

$$
\begin{array}{r}
2 \quad \bullet\bullet \\
+\,3 \quad \bullet\bullet\bullet \\
\hline
\end{array}
$$

Step 3.   count the dots and enter the answer:

$$
\begin{array}{r}
2 \quad \bullet\bullet \\
+\,3 \quad \bullet\bullet\bullet \\
\hline
5 \\
\end{array}
$$

Forward Chaining

Level 1:   set out the problem (Step 1)

e.g. 'what is 2 + 3?' becomes

$$
\begin{array}{r}
2 \\
+\,3 \\
\hline
\end{array}
$$

Level 2:   set out the problem (Step 1), and enter dots (Step 2)

e.g. 'what is 2 + 3?' becomes

```
      2  and then      2  • •
    + 3              + 3  • • •
    ___              ___
```

Level 3:   set out the problem (Step 1), enter dots (Step 2), count dots and enter the answer (Step 3)
e.g. 'what is 2 + 3?' becomes

```
   2  and then      2  • •      and then      2  • •
 + 3              + 3  • • •                 + 3  • • •
 ___              ___                          5
```

Backward Chaining

Level 1:   count dots and enter the answer (Step 3)
e.g.

```
              2  • •      becomes      2  • •
            + 3  • • •                + 3  • • •
            ___                         5
```

Level 2:   enter dots (Step 2), count dots and enter the answer (Step 3)
e.g.

```
   2  becomes      2  • •      and then      2  • •
 + 3             + 3  • • •                 + 3  • • •
 ___             ___                          5
```

Level 3:   set out the problem (Step 1), enter dots (Step 2), count dots and enter the answer (Step 3)
e.g. 'what is 2 + 3?' becomes

```
   2  and then      2  • •      and then      2  • •
 + 3             + 3  • • •                 + 3  • • •
 ___             ___                          5
```

In some cases, any of these three techniques may be appropriate. In others, a particular technique may be best suited, while another may be difficult to implement. The instructor must carefully evaluate which of these methods is most compatible with the practical requirements of the learning situation.

MORE COMPLEX RULES

The chains discussed so far are composed of simple steps, and progress through the chain follows a single, non-repeated path. Complex rules and procedures are somewhat more difficult to describe. The elements themselves may be of greater complexity, as may movement through the chain. Let us consider the example of long division. A procedure for long division appropriate for two-digit divisors is set out below:

Sample problem:

$$
\begin{array}{r}
21.3 \\
36\ \overline{)768.0} \\
-72 \\
\hline
48 \\
-36 \\
\hline
120 \\
-108 \\
\hline
12 \\
\end{array}
$$

Procedure:

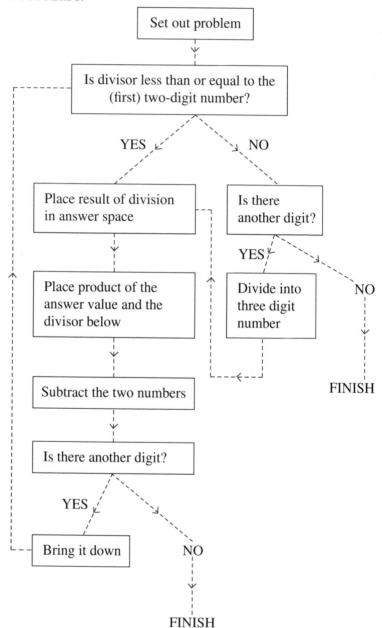

Sample steps:

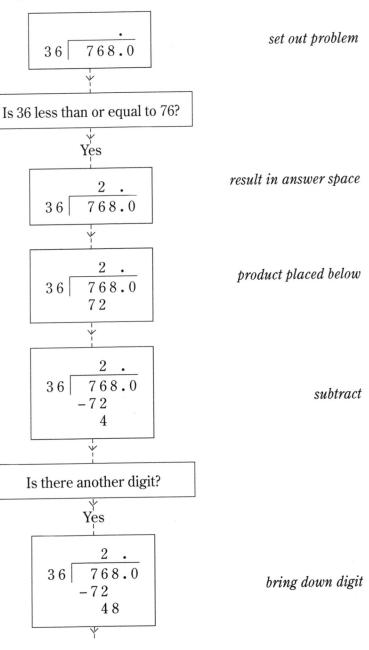

set out problem

Is 36 less than or equal to 76?

Yes

result in answer space

product placed below

subtract

Is there another digit?

Yes

bring down digit

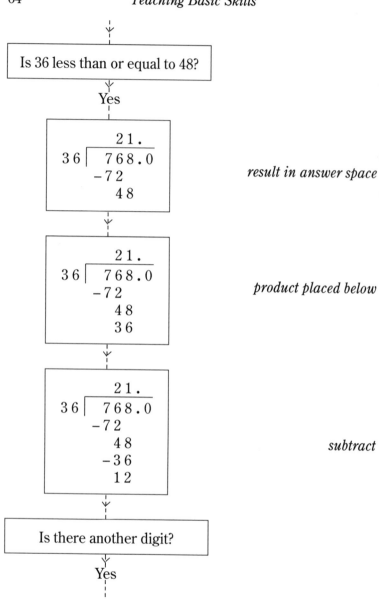

Is 36 less than or equal to 48?

Yes

```
        2 1 .
  3 6 | 7 6 8 . 0
       − 7 2
          4 8
```

result in answer space

```
        2 1 .
  3 6 | 7 6 8 . 0
       − 7 2
          4 8
          3 6
```

product placed below

```
        2 1 .
  3 6 | 7 6 8 . 0
       − 7 2
          4 8
       − 3 6
          1 2
```

subtract

Is there another digit?

Yes

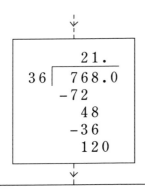

bring down digit

Is 36 less than or equal to 12?

No

Is there another digit?

Yes

```
       2 1 . 3
 3 6 │ 7 6 8 . 0
     - 7 2
         4 8
       - 3 6
       1 2 0
```

result in answer space

```
       2 1 . 3
 3 6 │ 7 6 8 . 0
     - 7 2
         4 8
       - 3 6
       1 2 0
       1 0 8
```

product placed below

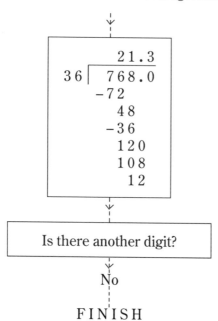

subtract

Is there another digit?

No

FINISH

With these complex chains, it is very important that the student is competent with the various components (e.g., discrimination of more or less, subtraction, multiplication, etc.) before putting them together into the chain. The various chaining techniques discussed above can be adapted for teaching the component skills that can later be used for teaching complex tasks such as long division. It can be seen from these examples how learning of basic skills to mastery level provides the basis for the development of much more sophisticated academic repertoires.

Shaping

Although often taken for granted, skills such as handwriting and speaking are important basic academic activities. For these and other production skills (e.g., various physical activities), shaping is an important instructional technique. Shaping involves gradual modification of the physical form of the behaviour so that it approaches the target level of performance (Becker, Engelmann & Thomas, 1975).

The first step in shaping is to identify the particular aspect of behaviour that needs to be developed. This may be the roundness of the letter *o*, the speed a person runs, the loudness of a person's voice in conversation with others, etc. In some cases, there will be several such aspects or dimensions of behaviour that need to be changed. For example, with the letter *o* its roundness, its size and its proximity to the line on which it is written may all need to be modified. Sometimes it may be possible to modify several things simultaneously, but it is generally easier to concentrate on one aspect at a time.

Shaping relies upon the fact that there is always a reasonable degree of variability in performance. Thus, if the particular skill or behaviour is observed on several occasions, it will be noted that some instances more closely approach the target level of performance than others. For example, if a student is asked to draw several instances of the letter *o*, some will more closely approximate the desired shape or size than others. Similarly, some will be closer to the line than others.

In shaping, the instructor begins by reinforcing those instances that most closely resemble the target level. Thus, there needs to be some criterion, the attainment of which leads to positive feedback. This may mean that in the early stages of shaping the instructor may actually be reinforcing behaviour which is quite different from the target. For example, if a student speaks too softly, then the instructor might begin by reinforcing occasional louder utterances even though they may still be barely audible. If the positive feedback has been chosen appropriately, these louder utterances should become more frequent. In fact, the overall voice loudness should increase. Once this has begun to occur, the criterion for positive feedback should be raised a little further toward the target level. This process is repeated until the target level is reached. Thus, the process is one of giving positive feedback to successive approximations of the target.

In some cases, there is a clear continuum from the starting level to the target level. For example, a student may write letters in very large print, but the target may be a much smaller size. Letter size can be shaped along a continuum from large to small. There are, however, instances where there is no such continuity. For example, students learning a second language may have to produce sounds not used in their native tongue. Following some initial modelling, the production of these sounds may be shaped by the instructor. The student's initial attempts may seem in no way similar to the desired sound. Nevertheless, the instructor must selectively reinforce those sounds that best approximate the target. In examples such as this one, the successive criteria used cannot be specified precisely. Instead, the process is dependent on the expert judgement of the instructor.

The main difficulty in shaping is associated with judgement of when to raise the criterion and by how much (Reese, 1966). If the criterion is raised too quickly or by too great an amount, the instructor may be placing demands on students which they cannot meet. If this occurs, the instructor will find that there are no instances of this criterion being met and, consequently, the instructor will find it necessary to drop the criterion back. As is generally the case with structured progression, the number and size of steps is dependent upon the difficulty of the task for the student. With shaping, the more difficult the task, the smaller the amount by which the criterion is increased each time. For students learning to write their first letter, shaping will involve a number of small increments in the criterion. As they learn more and more letters, this process can be accelerated.

Chapters 3 and 4 have demonstrated means by which instruction can be organized to ensure structured progression. In most instances, the prompts described in Chapter 3 will be combined with one of the methods described in this chapter. Examples of this have already been given in the chapter, and others will be provided in Chapter 5.

Choosing Between Procedures

There is one other issue to consider in the broader educational context. While there are many cases in which only one of the procedures described in this chapter will be appropriate, there are also many instances in which more than one alternative exists. The instructor then has to decide on the teaching method to be adopted. One obvious example of this is in the teaching of what are frequently called simple concepts such as geometric shapes. One approach would be to use the discrimination methods outlined. An alternative is to use a procedure which involves a sequence of logical steps that will allow the student to identify geometric shapes. This may be done by counting the number of sides and assessing angle values. To some extent the approach chosen is dependent on the instructor's individual style, with the choice being analogous to that between inductive and deductive approaches. The relative merits of each have been described elsewhere (e.g., Davis, Alexander & Yelon, 1974) and continue to be debated amongst educationists.

Chapter 4   Exercises
Try the following exercises. When you have completed them, check the answers at the end of the book.

1. For each of the three main techniques of errorless discrimination learning, illustrate a sequence of stimuli that could be presented to teach the discrimination between t and f.

2. For the first two techniques of errorless discrimination learning, illustrate a sequence of stimuli that could be presented to teach the discrimination between a larger and a smaller triangle.

3. Task analyse the following behaviours:
    (a) arranging any three numeral cards in ascending order
    (b) division of 23 by 5 to yield whole number and remainder
    (c) germinating seeds
    (d) applying a band-aid.

4. Describe how you would implement forward and backward chaining for the example in **3 (d)**.

5. Indicate how the following production skills might be shaped by considering questions such as —
    (a) what has to be modified
    (b) how performance is measured
    (c) the beginning and target levels
        (i)   writing letters of appropriate size (assume that the student can hold a pen and form letters, but the letters are too large)
        (ii) running faster (assume that the student can run competently)
        (iii) modifying length of presentation in 'show and tell' (assume that the student does not speak for long enough)

6. One other area in which shaping can be exploited is in the improvement of judgement skills. Indicate how shaping might be applied to improving a student's judgement of heights within the range of one to two metres.

Chapter 5
A sample instructional program

Previous chapters have explained a number of principles of instruction. These must be brought together when designing an instructional program. In this chapter this is done by using an example that has been developed across earlier chapters: single-digit addition. There are, of course, a number of ways in which this could be set out and a number of methods which could be used. What is outlined here is one way of doing it.

Mastery aim

— Student is able to enter correct answer to problems of addition of two single-digit numbers set out in the form
$x + y = ?$
— When presented with ten different problems of this type, the student should correctly answer eight. (This assumes that the student is going to continue with more problems of this type, thereby strengthening this skill. If, however, this was not going to happen, a criterion of nine out of ten may be more appropriate.)

Assumed Prerequisites

— Identification and naming of numerals 1 to 20
— Equivalence class for numerals 1 to 20*
— Counting by ones from any number in the range 1 to 9
— Can write numbers 1 to 20

> *This would normally occur in practice, but to do the problem of the exact type specified, only the relation between the written numeral and the set is required.

Types of learning

Discriminations:	signs + and =
Relations:	+ — 'plus'; = — 'equals'
Rules:	counting rule for addition

Instructional methods

DISCRIMINATIONS OF + AND = SIGNS

Mastery aim
Student is able **(a)** to name '+' (=) sign correctly and does not name other symbols as '+' (=) sign, and **(b)** to use this to read arithmetic sentences of the form $x + y$ ($x + y =$). Student should do **(a)** and **(b)** correctly for 9 out of 10 trials.

Method
We have chosen one way of teaching the '+' discrimination which would be appropriate for most normal children. However, a number of alternatives are possible. Set out below is a sequence of trials indicating the prompts, stimuli and feedback used:

Prompt/Question	Stimuli	Feedback
1. 'This is the plus sign'; points to + sign for about 4 seconds; removes pointer; 'show me the plus sign'.	○ +	'Well done, that is the plus sign' or 'No, this is the plus sign; it looks like this' (pointing to shape).
2. 'This is the plus sign'; points to + sign for	+ △	'Well done, that is it' or

Prompt/Question	**Stimuli**	**Feedback**
about 2–3 seconds; removes pointer; 'show me the plus sign'.		As above.
3. 'This is the plus'; points to + sign for about 2 seconds; removes pointer; 'show me it'.	$+$ ▭	'Great' or As above.
4. Points to + sign for about 1 second; removes pointer; 'show me the plus.'	$=$ $+$	'Well done' or As above.
5. 'Show me the plus.'	$+$ $-$	'Very good' or As above.
6. 'Point to the plus.'	$\div$ $+$	'Well done' or As above.
7. 'Which is the plus.'	$+$ $\div$	'That is good' or As above.
8. 'Show me the plus.'	$\times$ $+$	'Great' or As above.
9. 'Which is the plus.'	$\times$ $+$	'Very well done' or As above.

Note: Following an error, give feedback indicated and revert to previous trial.

— Following several errors within the space of a few trials, revert to the beginning of the program and have two trials at each level. If the student is still unsuccessful, employ a matching-to-sample approach.

With the instructions and feedback altered appropriately, the same instructions can be used to teach the '=' discrimination. The stimulus pairs could be as follows:

1.   =   ○

2.   =   △

3.   ✕   =

4.   ═   □

5.   ÷   =

6.   □   ═

7.   ═   —

8.   ═   ≠

9.   ≠   =

The final stage of teaching the '+' and '=' discriminations could be as presented below:

Question	Stimuli	Feedback
'What does this say?'; points to + sign.	+	'Great, that is the plus' or 'No, this is the plus — say plus.'
'What does this say?'; points to = sign.	=	'Very good, that is the equals' or 'No, this is equals — say equals.'

Repeat these trials in random order until the student gets 9 out of 10 correct. (If the student makes 3 errors in the first 10 trials, return to the start of the training sequence.)

'What does this say?'; points to equation.	5 + 3 =	'Well done.'
'What does this say?'; points to equation.	3 + 2 =	'Very good.'

Repeat trials like this until the student gets 9 out of 10 correct. (If the student gets the first 5 correct, it may be sufficient to stop at this point.)

At this stage, the student can read the written form of the problem. The student will now have to be taught the sequence of steps in solving problems of this type. There are several alternative procedures that can be used. One way is to use sets so that the student begins with problems of the type —

:   :   ⋮

•   +   =   •• and progresses to standard arithmetic problems like those above. However, as indicated in the prerequisites, it is assumed here that the student has learned the equivalence class for numerals 1 to 20. Thus, the student should have a good conceptual grasp of the processes involved when using the numerals only.

RULES: COUNTING RULE FOR ADDITION

Mastery aim
In response to + sign, the student is able to begin counting from the numeral preceding the sign by a number of units equal to the numeral following the sign. The student should do this correctly for 9 out of 10 problems.

Method
The sequence of steps in the task analysis is set out below, for the example 5 + 3 = . This would best be taught using total task presentation. All the prompts indicated would be used in the early trials, with a variety of examples.

Prompt/Question	Steps
1. Point to 3. 'Count out the second number on your fingers.'	Counts out 3 on fingers; that is, student is holding up 3 fingers.
2. Models three fingers held up. Points to 5 'What is the first number?'	Says 'five'

3. 'Count on from five until all your fingers are down — like this.' Models counting until all three fingers are down. 'Now start from five, and you do it.'	Counts 'six', 'seven', 'eight', bringing down a finger as each number is counted until all fingers are down.
4. 'What number did you reach?'	Says 'eight'
5. 'That is the number, write it down here.' Points to answer box.	Writes 8

Feedback

For all steps this is likely to be very similar. If the student is correct, some form of verbal praise is provided. If incorrect, the student is asked to attempt the step again. Only after two incorrect attempts is the student told the correct answer. This is because the student has already learned each of these component skills as part of the prerequisites.

Fading of prompts

Once the student has successfully tried several examples, the fading of prompts can begin. This could be done in the following stages, with the rate depending upon the student's progress.

Stage 1 step 1 : eliminate pointing (use prompt delay if necessary)

step 2 : eliminate pointing (use prompt delay if necessary)

step 3 : omit model counting on occasional trials and eventually eliminate

step 4 : eliminate pointing (use prompt delay if necessary)

Stage 2   step 1   :   abbreviate instruction: e.g. 'count the second number'

            step 2   :   omit model of correct number of fingers on occasional trials, and eventually eliminate

            step 3   :   abbreviate instruction: e.g. 'count from there'

            step 4   :   abbreviate question: e.g. 'what is the number?'

            step 5   :   abbreviate instruction: e.g. 'write it down'

Stage 3   occasionally and unpredictably omit one or more instructions until all prompts are eliminated.

By this stage, reinforcement for each step should also be occurring less frequently and unpredictably. Once all the prompts have been eliminated, the aim should be to rely only on feedback and reinforcement at the end of the whole problem. At this point it will be necessary to have feedback which indicates where the student made a mistake, rather than just indicating whether they are right or wrong.

This is obviously only the preliminary stage in learning addition. Eventually, self-generated prompts such as using fingers will need to be eliminated. This could be done using similar methods to those employed with external prompts.

PROBLEMS OF IMPLEMENTATION

Experience shows that instruction does not always progress smoothly. A variety of factors may contribute to day-to-day variability in student performance. Factors such as the individual's affective state and physiological and psychological changes induced by fatigue or environmental stressors may all contribute to this performance variability. The net effect of such variability is that progress on programs such as those described, or on those that you may devise, may sometimes be slower or more erratic than anticipated.

Chapter 6
Adaptations for students with learning problems

The preceding chapters describe a set of instructional principles for the teaching of basic academic skills. Three major aspects of instruction were emphasized: feedback, mastery and structured progression. For each of these aspects a number of principles were discussed and illustrated. The aim was to produce instruction which was efficient and organized in a way that leads to further understanding. Another aim was to promote methods which enable all students to learn. However, although the general methods outlined should enable most students to learn, there may be some students who will have difficulty and will require specifically designed instruction.

Most instructors will at some stage confront students who perform well below expectations in one particular area of instruction, but not in others. For example, some students display particular weaknesses in mathematics or reading or physical activities, but learning in other areas proceeds efficiently. It may have been the case with such students that learning of basic discriminations, relations, or rules and procedures, etc. did not even approach mastery levels, with the result that subsequent learning in that area was impeded. This, of course, will have led to the student falling progressively further behind. As indicated in Chapter 1, students cannot be expected to attain a particular level of conceptual understanding unless they have the appropriate prerequisites. For such students, instruction in problem areas should focus on those prerequisites not already mastered. Once this mastery has been achieved, the student can then work systematically through further prerequisites to more advanced levels. For these students, it is imperative that the methods outlined in earlier chapters be implemented systematically and comprehensively. This can mean the difference between learning and not learning. In addition, some of the approaches used when dealing with students who have more general learning problems could also be implemented. These are the focus of the rest of this chapter.

A number of students show more general learning problems, with difficulties occurring irrespective of the type of material being learned. For some individuals, these difficulties may be relatively mild. For others, the learning problems may be severe and recognizable before instruction begins. These general learning problems can be classified in terms of the clinical categories of intellectual disability (e.g., mild, moderate, severe etc.).

For students with these general learning problems, it is also imperative that the methods outlined earlier in this text are followed carefully. Frequently, however, these methods will require adaptation. In the remainder of this chapter the important adaptations that may be needed with students with intellectual disabilities will be described. (In some cases, such as shaping, the way the technique is used with intellectually disabled students does not differ from that described in earlier chapters.)

Feedback

Consistent feedback is essential for students with learning problems. However, when dealing with individuals who have severe, general, learning problems, incorporating all the elements of effective instructional feedback outlined in Chapter 2 (e.g., providing an ideal answer, highlighting the differences between the student answer and the ideal) will not be appropriate. This is because such students are unable to take in information as rapidly (Brewer, 1987; Maisto &

Baumeister, 1984; Spitz, 1973) and, furthermore, are un-likely to remember much of the presented information (Campione & Brown, 1977; Detterman, 1979). For these students, instructional feedback should be presented in a simple form. In the example in Question **1** (i) from Chapter 2 Exercises, the instructional feedback given to an individual with severe intellectual disability might be modified as in the table below. More detailed feedback, as is typically given to more able students, should not be used as it may lead to confusion.

Table 6.1

| Correct answer: | 'Yes, that is the square.' |
| Incorrect answer: | 'No, this is the square' (pointing to the square). |

There are also important considerations when providing motivational feedback to individuals with general learning problems. Many students are motivated by the achievement of some goal — for example, mastery of or competence in some activity. However, intellectually disabled students are less likely to be motivated in this way (Balla & Zigler, 1979; Zigler & Balla, 1982). Therefore, for these individuals, learning will be much more dependent on the provision of alternative or additional reinforcers. It is important that appropriate reinforcers are selected. One particular difficulty with intellectually disabled students, however, is that they do not express their preferences so clearly and the reinforcers chosen by a third person are frequently inappropriate (Green et al., 1988; Wacker, Berg, Wiggins, Muldoon & Cavanaugh, 1985). Accordingly, monitoring the effectiveness of reinforcement is of critical importance. If a potential reinforcer proves to be ineffective, more careful observation of a person's activities may be necessary to select a new reinforcer.

Generalization to novel contexts is often a major difficulty for intellectually disabled individuals (Borkowski & Cavanaugh, 1979; Stokes & Baer, 1977). That is, relatively small changes in the task or setting may produce a marked disruption in performance. Often, in fact, intellectually disabled individuals will show no generalization from one context to another. This is particularly the case with more severely disabled individuals. For this reason, instructors should be careful to ensure that the student is given appropriate feedback in a variety of contexts, with these being increasingly different from the original learning context. Even then, however, it may be difficult to establish generalization with some students.

In Chapter 2 it was indicated that generalization and feedback withdrawal are made easier if the student monitors his or her own performance. Whereas most students are likely to rehearse the various steps involved in a task spontaneously, it is unlikely that the intellectually disabled student will do this (Campione & Brown, 1977; Detterman, 1979). With such students, effective instruction in self-monitoring requires analysis of the procedure involved, instruction appropriate for that procedure, and careful monitoring of the student's performance following the initial instruction (Litrownik, 1982). In order for the instructor to be able to monitor the student's performance and give appropriate feedback, this self-monitoring will, at least initially, have to be overt. Thus, for students with intellectual disabilities, self-monitoring is learned in the same way as any other rule or procedure.

Mastery

When dealing with most students who have learning problems, a major difficulty is posed by their memory limitations. For example, they are less likely to employ, or to employ efficiently, strategies such as rehearsal and clustering which facilitate the memorizing and recall of information (Campione & Brown, 1977; Evans & Bilsky, 1979).

The implications of this are twofold. Firstly, such students should be trained to use appropriate strategies. The methods that can be used to do this with intellectually disabled individuals are beyond the scope of this book, but are discussed in Borkowski and Cavanaugh (1979), Campione and Brown (1977) and Evans and Bilsky (1979). Secondly, because these strategies are employed less efficiently if at all, the student will show a slower rate of improvement. As a result, more trials will be required to reach the same level of performance. It follows, therefore, that mastery aims for students with general learning problems will be less ambitious. Since the student's rate of progress is likely to be less, the mastery aims within a fixed instructional period will be more limited.

While such students will require more trials to reach a given level of performance, the criterion for progression should not be any stricter than that used with other students. It may even be less strict, as people with intellectual disabilities tend to display much greater than average variability in performance in a range of tasks (Baumeister, 1968). The instructor should therefore expect that inexplicable errors will arise from time to time, and take account of this in setting criteria.

PROMPTING AND FADING

Some of the prompts described in Chapter 3 may need to be implemented differently for students with intellectual disabilities. The more important of these differences are outlined here.

Instructions will need to be modified in a manner similar to that described in the section on instructional feedback above. That is, the instructions which are presented should be simpler and clearer, and presentation should be slower. Again, these adaptations are required because of the limitations in information input and memory characteristic of intellectual disability. One consequence is that instructors may rely less on instructions as a method of prompting.

There are grounds, however, for arguing that actually teaching self-instruction may result in considerable gains in retarded individuals' performance (Whitman, 1987). This is not surprising, given the well-documented limitations (see earlier) of retarded individuals in spontaneous rehearsal of verbal information. Self-instruction, by its very nature, encourages the use of this particular memory strategy. Again, the methods for teaching these are beyond the scope of this book, but are based on much the same principles as those described here.

The use of a model as a prompt is also constrained by the same student limitations. Modelling should therefore be used only when the desired behaviour can be displayed in a clear and simple manner. Complex behaviours are unsuitable for modelling with intellectually disabled students.

Many students who have an intellectual disability also have motor disorders of varying severity (Grossman, 1983) or less efficient organization and control of movement (Davis, 1986). One consequence is that prompting in the form of physical guidance may be required more often. Skills which other students may learn by modelling may be learned by disabled students only with the use of physical guidance. Regardless of the prompt being used, fading should be a more gradual process with students who have learning problems. In principle, this is no different than what has been already described in Chapter 3. That is, the number of fading steps is dictated by the ability of the student to adapt to the changing prompt intensity.

ERRORLESS DISCRIMINATION LEARNING

In Chapter 4 the rationale for errorless discrimination learning methods was outlined. Minimizing errors is absolutely crucial for the student who has an intellectual disability. Many such students have a high expectancy of failure (Balla & Zigler, 1979), and when confronted with failure on a new task are likely to show evidence of learned helplessness

(Weisz, 1982). When this occurs, the student will seem to be less motivated to succeed at the task, and this is often reflected in reduced persistence. Learned helplessness can only be reversed if the student does achieve initial success. The advantage of errorless learning is that it ensures this initial success.

Another major advantage of these methods is that they tackle the attentional limitations of intellectually disabled students. It is well documented that these students are less likely to isolate and attend to the relevant dimension in a discrimination problem (Zeaman & House, 1963, 1979). In trial-and-error learning tasks, they frequently respond for long periods of time on the basis of irrelevant dimensions, thus showing no evidence of learning. This may occur because they enter the task with strong preferences for attending to particular dimensions such as colour, position, novelty, etc. (Zeaman & House, 1979). Similarly, in changing from one task to another (e.g., changing from a form discrimination to a colour discrimination), disabled students have great difficulty if the relevant dimension changes (Mercer & Snell, 1977). It is quite likely, therefore, that many of these students will never learn unless the principles and procedures described in Chapter 4 are followed carefully.

In summary then, errorless discrimination procedures do not require any particular adaptations for the student with general learning problems. What we have emphasized, however, is that the principles described in Chapter 4 are indispensable for these students.

CHAINING

Several times in this chapter attention has been drawn to the limitations of intellectually disabled students in inputting and remembering information. In the case of learning rules and procedures, this means that any one component cannot be too large. Thus, a task analysis for a disabled student may consist of a larger number of smaller components than would be the case for a more able student. The other reason for analyzing a task into a larger number of smaller steps is that prompts such as instructions and models need to be kept simple for the disabled student. The best way to do this may be to ensure that each step is small, and thus the associated instructions or modelling are relatively simple.

As an example, consider Question **3(d)** from Chapter 4 Exercises, a task analysis for applying a band-aid. The original task analysis (pp.98 & 99) had seven steps. For a student who is intellectually disabled, a more appropriate task analysis may be as follows:

Table 6.2

Step 1.	Open box
Step 2.	Remove sealed band-aid from box
Step 3.	Find 'tear-off' mark at end of band-aid
Step 4.	Grasp band-aid wrapper at this point
Step 5.	Tear off end of band-aid
Step 6.	Pull thread to open seal
Step 7.	Take band-aid from seal
Step 8.	Separate tabs and place gauze over cut
Step 9.	Holding one end, remove tab from other end
Step 10.	Press band-aid to skin
Step 11.	Remove other tab
Step 12.	Press band-aid to skin

It becomes apparent that, when instructing disabled students, some behaviours which normally would not be task analyzed at all may be broken down into components. For example, the usual instructional procedures for teaching a student to draw a box may simply involve presenting a model and instructing the student to copy it. For less able students, however, the sides may need to be copied one at a time, with each step being modelled (e.g., placing a ruler to form a right angle).

An additional consideration concerns the cues that prompt each step in the chain. For students with intellectual disabilities, these need to be made as clear as possible. This is because of attentional problems such as those described in the section on errorless discrimination learning.

Conclusion

Carefully following the principles set out in earlier chapters, and adapting them as indicated in this chapter, the instructor will be able to teach students with learning problems effectively. Learning will be slower, particularly in individuals with more severe learning problems, and performance probably will not reach the same level as in more able students. Nevertheless, appropriate use of the techniques will allow these students to develop skills that they would not otherwise attain.

Answers

Chapter 1

1. (i) relevant dimension   : shape: number of sides
                                    or points
   irrelevant dimensions : size, colour
   values of S+   : three-sided or three-
                                    pointed
   values of S−   : squares, circles etc.
   (ii) relevant dimension   : letter sound
   irrelevant dimensions : pitch, loudness
   values of S+   : 's'
   values of S−   : all other letter sounds
                                    and non-letter sounds.
   (iii) relevant dimension   : orthographic structure
                                    or form
   irrelevant dimensions : size, number of letters,
                                    first letter
   values of S+   : **'the'**, 'THE', 'the'
   values of S−   : any other word or other
                                    collections of letters.

2. **(a)** major stimulus classes : spoken   ('computer')
                                    written (computer)
                                    visual   (actual
                                            computer,
                                            representation
                                            of computer)

(b) all possible relations:

      'computer'   computer

'computer' computer [computer icon]	'computer' — computer computer — 'computer' [computer icon] — 'computer' [computer icon] — computer	'computer' — [computer icon] computer — [computer icon]

(c) There are two relations to be taught. From the six shown in the table, three can be eliminated because they are simply reversals of the other three (i.e. those above or those below the diagonal). However, once two of these are learned, the third will follow automatically and thus not require specific teaching.

(d) the likely order is —

    (i) [computer icon] — 'computer'

        Most students will have heard the word 'computer', and have seen one or a representation of one.

    (ii) computer — 'computer'

        The written form will usually be the most difficult to learn. This will generally be done in association with the spoken form.

3. (a) begin the sentence with an upper case letter and end it with a full stop or period.

    (b) for two, add 'er' (e.g. slower); for three or more, add 'est' (e.g. slowest).

    (c) use a conjunction (and, or, but, for, yet, so, nor) preceded by a comma.

4. There are several possible rules. Two of these are —

    (i) count upwards from the first number, a number of units equal to the second number: the number reached is the answer.

(ii) write down a number of dots corresponding to the first number, do likewise for the second number, and count the total number of dots to get the answer.

5. (i) production skill: articulate numbers 1 to 10
rule: 2 follows 1, 3 follows 2, etc.

(ii) production skill: articulate word and 'ess' sound
rule: add 'ess' sound to end of word.

(iii) production skill: depress key with appropriate pressure and release it.
rule: depress key corresponding to first letter of name, release, depress key corresponding to second letter of name, release, etc.

Chapter 2

1. (i) correct answer   : Yes, that is the square
incorrect answer : No, this is the square (pointing to square). The square has four sides/corners/points. The one you picked has three.
optionally   : Next time, count the number of sides/corners/points first.

(ii) correct answer   : Right, it is five.
incorrect answer : (where student has counted aloud four more than two). No, two plus three is five. You should count on three after two, not four.

(iii) correct answer   : Yes, you have started your sentence with a capital letter.
incorrect answer : No, you began with a small j. You should begin with a capital J like this (write over the top of his letter).

2. It is not possible to provide precise feedback for this question. However, as a guide, here are possible reinforcers for a typical instructional setting; e.g., a regular classroom for 6- to 7-year-olds.

— teacher praise, verbal and written (e.g., well done, good work)
— teacher attention
— teacher acknowledgement (facial expression, gestures)
— awards (stamps, stars)
— peer praise and attention
— access to games, books
— classroom duties (feeding classroom pets, running messages)
— time for favourite schoolwork
— opportunity to help other students with work
— group activities (outings)
— possibly tangible awards.

3. (i) **(a)** Praise can take several forms. Examples of instructional feedback with praise are —
Great, that is the square.
Very good, you picked the right one.

   (b) The student is consistently picking the desired shape; that is, on 5 to 6 consecutive occasions.

   (c) Initially, the praise would be given occasionally and unpredictably. Thus, on most occasions the feedback would be instructional only, as in **1** (i). Then, the instructional feedback would be reduced in frequency so that, as long as the student continues to be right, feedback would only come after several problems have been solved.
   During this stage, the types of problem would be varied. For example, shapes of different colour, materials, etc. would be introduced.

   (ii) **(a)** Well done, five is exactly right.
   Excellent, you got it right again.

   (b) The student is consistently getting correct answers on single-digit addition problems of this standard; that is, on 5 to 6 consecutive problems.

(c) For feedback withdrawal, see **3** (i) **(c)**.

At this stage, the manner of presentation of problems would also be varied. For example, problems would be presented on the board, on paper, arranged horizontally, etc.

4. The student —
  (i) can give money value of any coin or note
  (ii) begins sentence with a capital letter
  ends sentence with a full stop or period
  uses commas before conjunctions and to separate items in a list
  does not use commas unnecessarily (e.g., between subject and verb)
  uses question marks at end of a question
  (iii) identifies which of two groups contains 'more' elements for —
  (a) a range of group sizes (e.g., 1 to 20)
  (b) different group elements (e.g., apples, shoes, dots)
  (c) differences of varying magnitude (e.g., 1 more, 5 more)
  (iv) reproduces lyrics accurately
  — sings in key and follows tune
  — modulates volume in response to direction
  — addresses audience.

Chapter 3

1. (a) 'Place the ruler below/on the paper so that it is even with the bottom/top of the paper all the way along. Move the ruler so that the 0 mark lines up with the left hand side of the paper. Read the number that lines up with the right hand side of the paper.'

(b) 'Write down the first number. Write the second number directly underneath it. Put a plus sign next to (on the left hand side of) the second number. Draw a line underneath the plus sign and second number.'

2. Ideally — the model should carry through the whole procedure of taking the disk out of its sleeve, orienting it correctly, placing it in the drive and closing the drive.

   — the best model would be someone actually doing this, rather than a video, pictorial representation, etc.

   — the best person to carry this out would be a peer who is liked and respected by the audience.

   — the modelling should be slow and careful enough so that the student can correctly observe the orientation of the disk, where it is placed, etc.

   — the student should be able to see a beneficial result of inserting the disk correctly (i.e., the computer can be used).

3. The student would be presented with a sample red object or shape, and an identical red object or shape together with several other objects or shapes of different colours. The student is asked to identify the one which is red, like 'this one'.

   Over a series of trials the instructor would vary the types of objects presented, the arrangement of objects, and the colour of incorrect objects. It is also important that, on a number of trials, the sample and the correct object are dissimilar in most respects.

4. **(a)** bold or point to the vertical downstroke on the *a*
   (b) bold or point to the vertical sides of the rectangle and the diagonal sides of the parallelogram

(c) highlight or point to the space between the pair (i.e., a small space vs. a large space).

5. (a) Either abbreviation of the instructions or prompt delay could be used.
One set of abbreviated instructions might be —
'Put the ruler below/on the paper. Line it up and read the answer.'
The two could also be combined. For example, the abbreviated instructions might only be given if the student fails to initiate the appropriate action within a certain period of time.

(b) In this particular example, the most appropriate way of fading modelling would be to use response delay as follows. On the student's first attempt, he or she would have the opportunity to do each step immediately after it was modelled. Then, a couple of steps may be modelled consecutively, imposing a greater delay between the prompted step and the student's attempt. Finally, all steps would be modelled, imposing an even greater delay. If necessary, a later stage could be added where there is a delay between the complete presentation of the modelled steps and the opportunity for the student to perform the task.

(c) Since fading intensity of the sample is not appropriate in this example (because it changes the colour), delayed matching would be used. That is, there is a gradually increasing delay from the end of the sample presentation period to the presentation of the stimuli.

(d) Gradually reduce the amount of bolding on the vertical downstroke of the *a*.

(e) Either prompt delay or response delay could be used here. In the former case, the instructor may ask the question, allow the student some time to respond, and then give the prompt if the student fails to answer. With successive correct answers, the instructor delays the prompt progressively until it is no longer required.

In the latter case, the instructor may briefly point to the critical aspects of the shape and then wait a short period before asking the student to identify it. This delay could be progressively increased before the prompt is eliminated.

Chapter 4

1.

	S+	S−
(i)	t	o
	t	n
	t	p
	t	j
	t	k
	t	f

	S+	S−
(ii)	t	
	t	⋮
	t	⦂
	t	⸬
	t	f
	t	f

	S+	S−
(iii)	t	'
	t	'
	t	r
	t	r
	t	f
	t	f

2.   S+   S–

(i)   △   •

             ◿   ◿

                          △

             △   △

             △   ◸

S+   S−

(ii)

3. (a) Step 1   Identify the lowest number
         Step 2   Place that card to one side

Step 3 Identify the smaller of the two remaining numbers

Step 4 Place that card at the right hand side of the first card

Step 5 Place the remaining card at the right hand side of the previous card.

(b) Step 1 Set out the problem

$$\begin{array}{r} R \\ 5\overline{\smash{)}23} \end{array} \quad \text{or} \quad \begin{array}{r} \blacksquare \\ 5\overline{\smash{)}23} \end{array}$$

Step 2 Divide 5 into 23

won't go

Step 3 Find the next lowest divisible by 5

20

Step 4 Divide that number by 5 and enter answer at the top

$$\begin{array}{r} 4\,R \\ 5\overline{\smash{)}23} \end{array} \quad \text{or} \quad \begin{array}{r} 4\,\blacksquare \\ 5\overline{\smash{)}23} \end{array}$$

Step 5 Subtract that number from 23 and enter the remainder at the top.

$$\begin{array}{r} 4\,R\,3 \\ 5\overline{\smash{)}23} \\ 20 \\ \hline 3 \end{array} \quad \text{or} \quad \begin{array}{r} 4\,\blacksquare\,3 \\ 5\overline{\smash{)}23} \\ 20 \\ \hline 3 \end{array}$$

(c) Step 1 Place several sheets of paper towel in a saucer

Step 2 Scatter seeds evenly over paper

Step 3 Sprinkle water onto seeds until paper is completely moistened

Step 4 Check paper daily — if starting to dry, remoisten.

(d) Step 1 Remove sealed band-aid from box

Step 2 Tear off end of band-aid (at marked end)

Step 3 Pull thread to open seal

Step 4   Take band-aid from seal
Step 5   Separate tabs and place gauze over cut
Step 6   Holding one end, remove tab from other
          end and press band-aid to skin
Step 7   Remove other tab and press to skin.

4. Forward chaining

Level 1:   student does Step 1 (remove band-aid) and
           instructor does Steps 2 to 7
Level 2:   student does Steps 1 & 2 (remove band-aid,
           tear end) and instructor does Steps 3 to 7
Level 3:   student does Steps 1 to 3 (remove .... pull
           thread) and instructor does Steps 4 to 7
Level 4:   student does Steps 1 to 4 (remove .... take
           from seal) and instructor does Steps 5 to 7
Level 5:   student does Steps 1 to 5 (remove ....
           place gauze) and instructor does Steps 6 to 7
Level 6:   student does Steps 1 to 6 (remove ....
           press on) and instructor does Step 7
Level 7:   student does Steps 1 to 7 (remove ....
           press other tab on).

Backward chaining

Level 1:   instructor does Steps 1 to 6, student does
           Step 7
Level 2:   instructor does Steps 1 to 5, student does
           Steps 6 to 7
Level 3:   instructor does Steps 1 to 4, student does
           Steps 5 to 7
Level 4:   instructor does Steps 1 to 3, student does
           Steps 4 to 7
Level 5:   instructor does Steps 1 to 2, student does
           Steps 3 to 7
Level 6:   instructor does Step 1, student does Steps 2 to
           7
Level 7:   student does Steps 1 to 7

5.   (i) In this case, the dimension to be changed is letter
          size as indicated by height. This would be

measured by determining the separation of lines within which the student can constrain letter height. After establishing what is the minimum height within which the student constrains his or her writing, any attempt of that height or less is reinforced from the outset. A target level should be set which matches the expected level for that age group. Once the student is being consistently reinforced at the beginning level, the separation of lines is reduced a little toward the target level. The separation is further reduced when the student is reinforced consistently at this new level, and this process continues until the target level is reached.

(ii) The dimension is speed of running, as measured by the time taken to run a set distance. The average time taken to run the distance over several attempts (or perhaps the minimum of three attempts) is measured and is used as the beginning criterion. Anything better than this will be reinforced. The target criterion will be determined by the instructor's assessment of a number of factors including child's build and physical prowess, time available for training and purpose of training. As before, a number of intervening targets are set, and the student progresses only after attaining consistent performance at each of these levels.

(iii) The dimension is length of presentation. In theory, the most appropriate measure would be number of words or complete sentences. Since this would generally be too difficult for an instructor to monitor, the most practical measure would be duration. Several presentations by the student would be timed and, again, either the average or some lower target would be used as the beginning criterion. The target criterion would be the duration required for the student to produce a presentation of desired length. While all student attempts will receive the standard acknowledgement, those which meet or exceed the criterion should be followed by some extra reinforcement (e.g., praise, added interest in the contents of the presentation, etc). Progress occurs as in the above examples.

6. In this example, the dimension is height, measured in centimetres. Performance can be measured by noting the percentage deviation from the correct value. The beginning level would then be set, allowing a certain percentage deviation in either direction. The exact figure could be based on factors such as the student's current performance, the instructor's knowledge of the accuracy of student judgements, etc. The target criterion would be similarly set, but would be a smaller percentage deviation. In between would be graduated steps, on each of which the student must perform consistently. Over a series of trials, the student would be required to judge various different heights.

Glossary

Chaining	Teaching a complex rule or procedure by division into sequential elements which are learned individually.
Consistency level	The relative frequency with which performance meets some specified standard.
Dimension	An attribute or characteristic of a stimulus or set of stimuli (e.g., colour, thickness, complexity). A dimension may be relevant to the task in hand (e.g., shape when learning geometric figures) or irrelevant (e.g., colour in the same task).
Discrimination	Differentiation among a group of stimuli, demonstrated by responding differently to each.
Equivalence class	The set of all possible relations among a group of stimulus classes.
Errorless learning	The performance of students when instruction is designed to ensure gradual progression with no or minimal errors.

Fading	Gradual reduction in the role of a prompt.
Feedback	Consequences of a behaviour which provide information about that behaviour and, possibly, some motivation for continuing or discontinuing.
Generalization	Maintaining learning beyond the conditions in which it first occurred (especially when the stimuli are slightly different from those originally used).
Known equivalent	A stimulus which is known by the student to be equivalent to the stimulus in question (i.e., the student has learned the relation between the two).
Mastery	Achievement of a specified standard.
Matching-to-sample	Task in which a sample stimulus is presented together with two or more choice stimuli. The student must select the choice stimulus which matches the sample in the appropriate way.
Model	A form of prompt in which the desired behaviour is demonstrated.
Operationalize	To specify in terms which describe the actual behaviour involved.
Pacing	Ensuring an appropriate rate

	of progression towards a learning goal.
Production skill	Physical act which must be learned through gradual improvement in performance (e.g., handwriting).
Prompting	Provision of an aid to solution of a problem (e.g., by use of a model or instructions).
Reinforcement	The delivery or provision of a reinforcer.
Reinforcer	An outcome or consequence of a behaviour that increases its future probability.
Relation	An equivalence between two stimuli (having the same meaning) (e.g., the written and spoken forms of a word).
Rule	Procedures which, if followed, produce a certain outcome; they vary from simple to multi-step.
S+	The correct stimulus, usually chosen from one or more alternatives.
S–	An incorrect stimulus.
Self-monitoring	Recording and evaluation of behaviour by the person engaged in it.
Shaping	Reinforcing successive approximations to a target level of performance by gradually raising the criterion.

Social reinforcement	Provision of reinforcers through social interaction (e.g., smile, statement of approval, etc.).
Stimulus class	A group or set of stimuli which share one or more characteristics (e.g., all triangles, all instances of the digit '3'.
Structured progression	Arrangement of learning so that successive tasks are of gradually increasing difficulty; designed to minimize errors.
Task analysis	Division of a complex rule or procedure into sequential elements.
Total task presentation	A method of chaining in which the student carries out the complete sequence with the aid of prompts which are then faded.

References

Adams, J.A. (1976). *Learning and memory: an introduction.* Homewood, IL: The Dorsey Press.

Alberto, P.A., & Troutman, A.C. (1986). *Applied behavior analysis for teachers* (2nd ed.). Columbus, OH: Charles E. Merrill.

Anastasi, A. (1990). *Psychological testing* (6th ed.). New York: Macmillan.

Balla, D., & Zigler, E. (1979). Personality development in retarded persons. In N.R. Ellis (Ed.), *Handbook of mental deficiency, psychological theory and research* (2nd ed., pp. 143–68). Hillsdale, N.J.: Lawrence Erlbaum.

Bandura, A. (1969). *Principles of behavior modification.* New York: Holt, Rinehart & Winston.

Bandura, A. (1971). *Social learning theory.* New York: McCaleb-Seiler.

Baumeister, A.A. (1968). Behavioral inadequacy and variability of performance. *American Journal of Mental Deficiency, 73*, pp. 477–83.

Becker, W.C., & Carnine, D.W. (1981). Direct instruction: a behavior theory model for comprehensive educational intervention with the disadvantaged. In S.W. Bijou & R. Ruiz (Eds.), *Behavior modification: contributions to education* (pp. 145–210). Hillsdale, N.J.: Lawrence Erlbaum.

Becker, W.C., Engelmann, S., & Thomas, D.R. (1975). *Teaching 2: Cognitive learning and instruction.* Chicago, IL: Science Research Associates.

Belmont, J.M., Butterfield, E.C., & Ferretti, R.P. (1982). To secure transfer of training instruct self-management skills. In D.K. Detterman & R.J. Sternberg (Eds.), *How and how much can intelligence be increased*. Norwood, N.J.: Ablex.

Block, J., & Burns, R. (1977). Mastery learning. In L. Shulman (Ed.), *Review of research in education* (Vol. 4). Itasca, IL: F.E. Peacock.

Borkowski, J.G., & Cavanaugh, J.C. (1979). Maintenance and generalization of skills and strategies by the retarded. In N.R. Ellis (Ed.), *Handbook of mental deficiency, psychological theory and research* (2nd ed., pp. 569–617). Hillsdale, N.J.: Lawrence Erlbaum.

Brewer, N. (1987). Processing speed, efficiency, and intelligence. In J.G. Borkowski & J.D. Day (Eds.), *Cognition in special children: comparative approaches to retardation, learning disabilities, and giftedness* (pp. 15–48). Norwood, N.J.: Ablex.

Campione, J.C., & Brown, A.L. (1977). Memory and metamemory development in educable retarded children. In R.V. Kail & J.W. Hagen (Eds.), *Perspectives on the development of memory and cognition* (pp. 367–406). Hillsdale, N.J.: Lawrence Erlbaum.

Davis, R.H., Alexander, L.T., & Yelon, S.L. (1974). *Learning system design*. New York: McGraw-Hill.

Davis, W.E. (1986). Development of coordination and control in the mentally handicapped. In H.T.A. Whiting & M.G. Wade (Eds.), *Themes in motor development* (pp. 143–58). Dordrecht: Martinus Nijhoff.

Detterman, D.K. (1979). Memory in the mentally retarded. In N.R. Ellis (Ed.), *Handbook of mental deficiency, psychological theory and research* (2nd ed., pp. 727–60). Hillsdale, N.J.: Lawrence Erlbaum.

Etzel, B.C., Le Blanc, J.M., Schilmoeller, K.J., Stella, M.E. (1981). Stimulus control procedures in the education of young children. In S.W. Bijou & R. Ruiz (Eds.), *Behavior modification: contributions to education* (pp. 3–37). Hillsdale, N.J.: Lawrence Erlbaum.

Evans, R.A., & Bilsky, L.H. (1979). Clustering and categorical list retention in the mentally retarded. In N.R. Ellis (Ed.), *Handbook of mental deficiency, psychological theory and research* (2nd ed., pp. 533–68). Hillsdale, N.J.: Lawrence Erlbaum.

Gagné, R.M., Briggs, L.J., & Wager, W.W. (1988). *Principles of instructional design* (3rd ed.). New York: Holt, Rinehart & Winston.

Glynn, E.L., Thomas, J.D., & Shee, S.M. (1973). Behavioral self-control of on-task behavior in an elementary classroom. *Journal of Applied Behavior Analysis, 6*, pp. 105–13.

Green, C.W., Reid, D.H., White, L.K., Halford, R.C., Brittain, D.P., & Gardner, S.M. (1988). Identifying reinforcers for persons with profound handicaps: staff opinion versus systematic assessment of preferences. *Journal of Applied Behavior Analysis, 21*, pp. 31–43.

Grossman, H.J. (1983). *Classification in mental retardation.* Washington, DC: American Association on Mental Deficiency.

Harter, S. (1983). Developmental perspectives on the self-system. In E.M. Hetherington (Ed.), *Handbook of child psychology: socialization, personality and social development* (Vol.4, pp. 278–386). New York: Wiley.

Haupt, E.J., Van Kirk, M.J., Terraciano, T. (1975). An inexpensive fading procedure to decrease errors and increase retention of number facts. In E. Ramb & G. Semb (Eds.), *Behavior analysis: areas of research and application* (pp. 225–32). Englewood Cliffs, N.J.: Prentice Hall.

House, B.J. (1982). Learning processes: developmental trends. In J. Worell (Ed.), *Psychological development in the elementary years* (pp. 187–232). New York: Academic Press.

Hyman, J.S., & Cohen, B.A. (1979). Learning for mastery: ten conclusions after 15 years and 3,000 schools. *Educational Leadership, 37*, pp. 104–9.

Kazdin, A.E. (1984). *Behavior modification in applied settings* (3rd ed.). Chicago, IL: The Dorsey Press.

Lancioni, G.E., & Smeets, P.M. (1986). Procedures and parameters of errorless discrimination training with developmentally impaired individuals. In N.R. Ellis & N.W. Bray (Eds.), *International review of research in mental retardation* (Vol.14, pp. 135–64). Orlando, FL: Academic Press.

Litrownik, A.J. (1982). Special considerations in the self-management training of the developmentally disabled. In P. Karoly & F.H. Kanfer (Eds.), *Self management and behavior change: from theory to practice* (pp. 315–52). New York: Pergamon.

Maisto, A., & Baumeister, A.A. (1984). Dissection of component processes in rapid information processing tasks: comparison of retarded and nonretarded people. In Brooks, P.H., Sperber, R., & McCauley, C. (Eds.), *Learning and cognition in the mentally retarded* (pp.165–88). Hillsdale, N.J.: Lawrence Erlbaum.

Martin, G., & Pear, J. (1983). *Behavior modification: what it is and how to do it* (2nd ed.). Englewood Cliffs, N.J.: Prentice Hall.

Meichenbaum, D.H. (1977). *Cognitive-behavior modification: an integrative approach.* New York: Plenum Press.

Mercer, C.D., & Snell, M.E. (1977). *Learning theory research in mental retardation: implications for teaching.* Columbus, OH: Charles E. Merrill.

O'Leary, K.D., & O'Leary, S.G. (Eds.) (1977). *Classroom management: the successful use of behavior modification* (2nd ed.). New York: Pergamon.

Reese, E.P. (1966). *The analysis of human operant behavior.* Dubuque, IA: William C. Brown.

Rosenbaum, M.S., & Drabman, R.S. (1979). Self-control training in the classroom: a review and critique. *Journal of Applied Behavior Analysis, 12,* pp. 467–85.

Ross, A.O. (1978). Behavior therapy with children. In S.L. Garfield & A.E. Burgin (Eds.), *Handbook of psychotherapy and behavior change: an empirical analysis* (pp. 591–620). New York: Wiley.

Salvia, J.M., & Ysseldyke, J.E. (1981). *Assessment in special and remedial education* (2nd ed.). Boston, MA: Houghton Mifflin.

Sattler, J.M. (1982). *Assessment of children's intelligence and special abilities* (rev. ed.). Boston, MA: Allyn & Bacon.

Sidman, M., & Tailby, W. (1982). Conditional discrimination vs. matching to sample: an expansion of the testing paradigm. *Journal of the Experimental Analysis of Behavior, 37*, pp. 5–22.

Spitz, H.H. (1973). The channel capacity of educable mental retardates. In D.K. Routh (Ed.), *The experimental psychology of mental retardation* (pp. 133–56). London: Crosby Lockwood Staples.

Stokes, T.F., & Baer, D.M. (1977). An implicit theory of generalization. *Journal of Applied Behavior Analysis, 10*, pp. 349–67.

Terrace, H.S. (1963a). Discrimination learning with and without errors. *Journal of the Experimental Analysis of Behavior, 6*, pp. 1–27.

Terrace, H.S. (1963b). Errorless transfer of a discrimination across two continua. *Journal of the Experimental Analysis of Behavior, 6*, pp. 223–32.

Trabasso, T.R., & Bower, G.H. (1968). *Attention in learning: theory and research*. New York: Wiley.

Wacker, D.P., Berg, W.K., Wiggins, B., Muldoon, M., & Cavanaugh, J. (1985). Evaluation of reinforcer preferences for profoundly handicapped students. *Journal of Applied Behavior Analysis, 18*, pp. 173–8.

Weiss, K.M. (1978). A comparison of forward and backward procedures for the acquisition of response chains in humans. *Journal of the Experimental Analysis of Behavior, 29*, pp. 255–9.

Weisz, J.R. (1982). Learned helplessness and the retarded child. In E. Zigler & D. Balla (Eds.), *Mental retardation, the developmental-difference controversy* (pp. 27–40). Hillsdale, N.J.: Lawrence Erlbaum.

Welford, A.T. (1976). *Skilled performance: perceptual and motor skills*. Glenview, IL: Scott Foresman.

White, R.W. (1959). Motivation reconsidered: the concept of competence. *Psychological Review, 66*, pp. 197–233.

Whitman, T.L. (1987). Self-instruction, individual differences, and mental retardation. *American Journal of Mental Deficiency, 92*, pp. 213–23.

Zeaman, D., & House, B.J. (1963). The role of attention in retardate discrimination learning. In N.R. Ellis (Ed.), *Handbook of mental deficiency* (pp. 159–223). New York: McGraw-Hill.

Zeaman, D. & House, B.J. (1979). A review of attention theory. In N.R. Ellis (Ed.), *Handbook of mental deficiency, psychological theory and research* (pp. 63–120). Hillsdale: N.J.: Lawrence Erlbaum.

Zigler, E., & Balla, D. (1982). Motivational and personality factors in the performance of the retarded. In E. Zigler & D. Balla (Eds.), *Mental retardation, the developmental-difference controversy* (pp. 9–26). Hillsdale, N.J.: Lawrence Erlbaum.

Index

acquisition 19, 22
attention 2–4, 55
  errorless learning 55
  for special populations 84
  use of highlighting 40–41

chaining 55–66
  backward 59
  feedback in 58–59
  forward 59
  prompting 58–59
  for special populations 84–86
  techniques of 58–66
conceptual understanding 10–11, 13, 24
  in sample program 75
consistency level 28–29

dimension 3–4, 50, 55
discriminations *see also* errorless learning 1–4, 7
  difficulty of 2
  in sample program 72–74
  for special populations 84
  use of matching-to-sample 37–38
  use of pointers 40

equivalence class 6–7, 41
  in sample program 75
errorless learning 49–55
  for special populations 83–84
  techniques of 50–55

fading 32, 41–47
  highlighting 46
  instructions 43–44, 47
  known equivalents 46
  matching to sample 45, 47
  methods of 43
  models 44–45, 47
  physical guidance 45, 47
  pointers 45–47
  prompt delay 43–45, 47
  response delay 43–45, 47
  in sample program 76–77
feedback *see also* reinforcer 13–23, 32, 34
  in chaining 58–59
  corrective 16, 19–21, 41
  delay 19–20
  instructional 14–16, 22
  for models 36
  motivational 16–19, 21–22
  positive 13
  role of 14–19
  in sample program 72–74, 76–77
  in shaping 67
  for special populations 79–81

generalization 22
  for special populations 81

highlighting 40–41

identification 1

instructions 32–34
  in sample program 73
  for special populations 82–83
intellectual disability 79–86
  attentional limitations 84
  chaining for 84–86
  discrimination learning in 84
  errorless discrimination
   learning for 83–84
  feedback for 79–81
  generalization in 81
  instructions for 82–83
  learned helplessness in 83–84
  mastery for 81–86
  models for 83
  prompting and fading for
   82–83
  reinforcers for 80
  self-instruction for 83
  task analysis for 84–85

known equivalent 41

mastery *see also* mastery aims 13,
  23–29
  for special populations 81–86
mastery aims *see also* mastery
  25–26
  in sample program 71–72, 75
  special populations 82
matching-to-sample 37–38
  delayed matching 45
  in sample program 73
metacognitive training 34
model 15, 34–36
  nature of 35–36
  for special populations 83
motor skills *see* production skills

naming 1–2

objectives 23–27
operationalize 26

pacing 27–29
  self-pacing 27
physical guidance 38–39
physical skills *see* production
  skills
pointers 40
procedures *see* rules
production skills 9–10
  shaping of 66
prompting 32–47
  chaining 58–59
  highlighting 40–41
  instructions 32–34
  known equivalents 41
  matching-to-sample 37–38
  models 34–36
  physical guidance 38–39
  pointers 40
  in sample program 72–73,
   75–77
  for special populations 82–83

reinforcement *see* reinforcer
reinforcer *see also* feedback 16–20
  criticisms of 18–19
  favourite activity 17
  magnitude 18
  natural 18
  progression 16
  selection of 17–18
  in sample program 77
  in shaping 67
  social 17
  for special populations 80
  withdrawal of 20–21
relation 4–7
  use of matching-to-sample
   37–38
  in sample program 72
rules 7–9, 33, 55–58
  complex 61–66
  higher-order 8–9
  in sample program 72, 75

use of pointers 40
self-instruction 34
   for special populations 83
self-monitoring 21–23
self-motivation 16
shaping 10, 66–69
   criterion for 68
   reinforcement in 67
special populations 78–86
   chaining for 84–86
   errorless discrimination
      learning for 83–84
   feedback for 79–81
   generalization in 81
   instructions for 82–83
   learned helplessness in 83–84

mastery for 81–86
memory in 81
models for 83
prompting and fading for 82–83
reinforcers for 80
self-instruction for 83
stimulus class 4–6
structured progression 31, 49, 55,
   68
   minimization of errors 31–32

task analysis 56–58
   in sample program 75
   for special populations 84–85
total task presentation 58–59
   in sample program 75